LEWIS
9/12

3 JULY 19

Please return/renew this item by the last date shown

A GREEN GUIDE TO TRADITIONAL

COUNTRY FOODS

A GREEN GUIDE TO TRADITIONAL
COUNTRY FOODS

Discover traditional ways to cure and smoke,
pickle and preserve, make cheese, bake and more

GENERAL EDITOR HENRIETTA GREEN

Additional text by Jenny Linford

CICO BOOKS
LONDON NEW YORK
www.cicobooks.com

Published in 2011 by CICO Books
An imprint of Ryland Peters & Small Ltd
20–21 Jockey's Fields
London WC1R 4BW

10 9 8 7 6 5 4 3 2 1

www.cicobooks.com

Text, design and photography © CICO Books 2011
For recipe credits see page 192

ISBN: 978 1 907563 16 4

Printed in China

Copy editors: Alison Bolus and Kay Halsey
Designer: Louise Leffler
For additional credits see page 192

Contents

Introduction

I have always believed that food, essential for our survival, is a mirror of our society. Why and how we prepared what we prepared to eat all those centuries ago provide fascinating insights into our social history. Look at the produce and you get a sense of how our lands were farmed, the types of livestock raised and the importance placed on certain foodstuffs.

Back then, the struggle for survival was paramount; think of when there was no electricity, no fridges or freezers, no tins or cans, the most basic of farm machinery and no means of over-wintering the livestock and you realise how our forefathers must have struggled. Most of the traditional country foods were based on preserving – by salting, curing, smoking, baking, pickling or drying – the seasonal gluts for the long cold dark days ahead.

Modern technology has allowed us to master preservation but although the motives may have changed, the crafts remain. Undoubtedly they have been adapted – salt, for example, is no longer used in such large quantities, with the resulting tastes more fitting for our subtle appetites – but the principles are still the same.

This book is a celebration of these food crafts, then and now, and the craftsmen and women who continue to practise them.

As I travel about the countryside meeting them, I never fail to be struck by their passion and dedication. Whether they are newcomers who have made the deliberate decision to move away from life in the city or families who have handed down their secrets from father to son over the generations, they all share a bond, a common interest and goal. It is a worthy one – the ambition to make 'The Best'.

Their life may still be tough but, by and large, they enjoy it. Most work extremely hard and their reward, believe it or not, comes from the satisfaction in producing good food, a 'job well done' and the pleasure of their customers' enjoyment. As we chat away, they reveal insights and an attention to details that are awe-inspiring and I never cease to wonder at their enthusiasm and generosity.

Glance through these pages and you will see how these men and women are happy to share their 'secrets', the techniques

Left: Cider vinegar maturing in an open jar covered with muslin
Right: The all-important kneading process
Far right: Butter being shaped before packaging

that transforms the ordinary into the extra-ordinary. Read our highlighted producer profiles and you will see what I mean. They talk about fussing over a product as if it were their child; recognising when it is ready by how it might feel in the hand, look in the pan or smell in the air. These are instinctive reactions that come through practice and awareness. To the craftsmen, it is second nature, to us these are skills to which we must aspire.

So when you start trying the recipes – making your very first soft cheese, for example – may I encourage you to not only buy the best ingredients (a good milk will transform the flavour) but to keep the faith. I remember my first cheeses, made in my larder years ago when I lived in Oxfordshire. Lumpy and exceptionally gritty, if only I had known then about handling the curds! But it is only by practising that you, too, will learn and hone your instincts.

If you need final encouragement, remember a recipe is no more than a set of instructions that tells you how to make or prepare something with virtually no allowances for techniques. This was struck home forcibly when I went to a cook-in. A group of about ten of us – all food or cookery writers – was given aprons, the same recipe for cheese soufflé and told to get started. Some beat egg whites forcibly, others more languidly; some worked meticulously and others were far more slapdash. As for the soufflés, if some puffed up perfectly, others sank in despair. Each one was different in taste, texture and appearance.

Your techniques are bound to vary from one day to the next as well as from any other cook. So if your fudge is not as smooth as silk the first time around – give it another whirl. Don't be put off. Think of the generations of craftsman who have gone before you. And above all else – enjoy.

Henrietta Green

of their craft, which means we can not only better understand their produce and appreciate its values, but also set about making it for ourselves. And if you're lucky enough to spend time with them discussing the merits (or de-merits) of one product against another, you soon come to realise just how many details, layers and stages can exist in creating, say, nothing more complex than a loaf of bread.

When I was just starting out in the world of food, I remember meeting a wise and particularly seasoned (forgive the pun) producer whose family had been curing hams that boasted several royal warrants. Not only did he invite me into his curing room and spend hours explaining the distinctions between the seemingly random ingredients, but he also told me of his guiding principle. 'Quality', he explained, 'is like a chain. And every link – from the breed of pig, how it is fed, reared, slaughtered and hung, to the ingredients of the cure, how long it is cured for and even how often it is turned in the cure – has to be strongly forged. Each one matters. Each one affects the eating quality. And it's true for any and every product you are attempting to produce.'

The links I have since added to my quality chain are passion and instinct. These are characteristics successful producers have in abundance but are difficult to pin down – a pity, as so often it is that very commitment and 'just knowing'

Left: Light and fluffy marshmallows, delicious when dipped in melted chocolate
Right: Lemon and ginger cordial, a comforting and soothing drink that is perfect when you have a cold

Chapter I

THE DAIRY

Since ancient times, dairy products have been an important source of food. Milk is a remarkably versatile foodstuff, which can be both drunk and used to make a large range of products. For thousands of years, man has domesticated grass-grazing ruminants such as cows, goats and sheep in order to use the protein-rich milk. In the West it is the cow, peacefully grazing on lush, green grass, that is the iconic image of a dairy animal.

For centuries, dairy animals were laboriously milked by hand – a process that is nowadays largely mechanised. In the period before refrigeration, however, valuable, labour-intensive milk was highly perishable, so ingenious ways were devised to transform it into a number of different dairy products, such as cheese, cream, butter and yoghurt. Making *cheese* was a way of transforming the nutritious milk into produce that was not only delicious in its own right, but could also be kept for longer than fresh milk. *Cream* is the fat-rich part of milk, which rises naturally to the surface in milk that hasn't been homogenised (that is, treated to disperse the fat evenly throughout the milk) or is nowadays separated by centrifugal force. Cream, in turn, is transformed into *butter* through churning, which removes most of its water content to leave behind the butterfat, which is valued for its flavour, texture and enhanced keeping qualities. Finally, *yoghurt*, which is created by fermenting milk, will thicken into a semi-solid foodstuff with a distinctive sour tang.

The dairy – a cool, often tiled room – was once where women worked. It was here that the farmer's wife or dairymaid turned the milk into dairy products. With industrialisation and mechanisation, however, we have largely lost touch with the centuries-old processes by which milk was transformed into other foods. Nevertheless, making your own soft cheese is both simple and satisfying, and taking cream and transforming it into butter is a wonderful piece of kitchen alchemy.

Cheese

It is thought that the discovery that liquid milk could be transformed into solid cheese dates back thousands of years. Early shepherds found that the milk they stored in animal stomach or hide containers had naturally curdled and formed a soft curd-like cheese.

Nowadays, many artisanal cheese makers prefer using 'raw' or unpasteurised milk, feeling that this produces a more flavourful and interesting cheese and is a better reflection of the origin of the milk.

Of all the dairy foods, cheese is the most varied. It is made by curdling milk by adding bacterial cultures and the acidulating agent rennet, which contains the enzyme rennin (also known as chymosin), which occurs naturally in the stomachs of mammals (lemon juice can also be used). The cheese maker then works with the curds to produce the cheese required. Many intricate factors, including the temperature and time to which the milk and curds are heated and how the moisture is extracted from the curds, go towards creating cheese.

There are literally hundreds of different cheeses, ranging in size, texture and flavour, from small, fresh, delicate soft cheeses – eaten when only a few days old – to huge, hard cheeses, such as cloth-bound, traditional Somerset Cheddar, firm-textured and with a long-lasting savoury finish, or blue-veined cheeses such as Stilton, with their characteristic salty-sweet tang. It is extraordinary to think that such diversity all starts with just one ingredient: milk, whether from cows, goats, sheep or even buffalo.

Professional cheese makers use starter cultures, made from a mixture of rennet and lactic acid bacteria. The resulting curdling process creates both soft curds (made from coagulated proteins called caseins) and whey (the remaining

Opposite left: The all-important maturing process to give Cheddar its distinct flavour
Opposite right: Butter being pressed by hand to remove any water
Right: Dorstone goat's cheese rolled in ash

Above: Perroche cheese from Neal's Yard Dairy

liquid part of the milk). The whey is drained from the curds, and these curds are then worked on in different ways to create a variety of cheeses. A young, velvety-textured goat's cheese, for example, is created by carefully ladling the curds into small moulds and allowing the curds to lightly drain under their own weight. Cheeses with a firmer texture are made by pouring the curds into moulds to mesh them together and then pressing in a cheese press. A way of shaping cheese that is characteristically British is the wrapping of muslin around large, moulded cheeses before setting them aside to ripen for several months. This technique is used to hold the cheese together as it matures, and develops texture and flavour, and is traditionally used in the making of farmhouse Cheddars.

One of the striking features of the cheese-making process is the way cheese makers work with bacteria, using it to affect the flavour, texture and aroma. Creating the right conditions in which to encourage the required bacteria to thrive and grow is part of the craft of cheese making. Different bacterial cultures are added to the milk at the beginning of the cheese-making process to create specific flavours and types of cheeses. In traditional Swiss cheese making, for example, a bacterium called *Propionibacteria shermanii*, also known as the 'hole-maker', creates carbon dioxide bubbles inside the cheese, which result in the holes characteristic of Emmental and other Swiss cheeses.

Blue cheeses, such as Stilton or Roquefort, are made by adding a bacterial culture called *Penicillium roqueforti* as a starter. In order to allow these bacteria to grow and thrive, these cheeses are never pressed, with the curd instead piled loosely into moulds. The bacteria turn blue-green in reaction to the air. To ensure this happens, the cheeses are pierced with long rods to let air enter the cheese, and the distinctive blue veining occurs.

Several types of cheeses may be brined in a salt solution while still very young (within 24 hours of making). Later on, another technique, washed rind, can come into play. This is done by wiping or soaking or washing the outside of the cheese with a bacteria, a salt solution or even an alcohol-based solution. As the natural bacteria grows, it creates a coating or skin on the cheese – think of the sticky orange-red outside of France's Epoisses, Ireland's Gubbeen or England's Stinking Bishop.

Meet the producer: Cothi Valley Goats

'My real passion is the goats,' admits Lynne Beard of Cothi Valley Goats who, together with her husband Richard, keeps 350 goats (a mixture of white-coated British Saanens and brown-coated British Toggenburgs) on her farm. 'They're so individual; no two goats are the same. They have a wicked sense of humour and can drive you round the bend, but they're beautiful.'

'Contented animals make for better produce,' observes Lynne, who ensures that her beloved goats lead as natural a life as possible. 'They forage outside from spring to autumn, though if it's wet, no goat will put its hoof outside the barn! They have access to a large yard all year round. We don't use any artificial daylight to trick them into producing milk; instead we have half the herd kid one year, the other half kid the next. That way I always have some goat milk to work with.'

The unpasteurised milk from their herd is turned by Lynne into seven different cheeses, ranging from Luddesdown, a soft, fresh cheese with a 'delicate, lemony, lactic' flavour, sold when just a few days old, to Tally Las, a month-old blue cheese, with a creamy texture and 'delicate' blue flavour.

'There's something very satisfying about making cheese using milk from your own animals; we don't use any bought-in milk. I know my animals are healthy and that the milk is safe. I prefer using unpasteurised milk as I feel it gives the cheeses a better flavour, more individuality and character. Everyone goes on about spring milk (milk from goats calved in the spring), but I love autumn milk. There's less of it, but it has a great fat and protein content that makes wonderful, velvety creamy cheese. I can feel the difference in the curd in autumn. Goat's milk curd is very delicate, so you have to treat it gently. You can't bash it about and you mustn't stir it too hard.'

The Beards then sell their cheeses direct at farmers' markets and food festivals. 'That's the good bit when, after all the hard work, and it is hard work, people come up and tell you how much they've enjoyed your cheese and you know what you're doing is appreciated.'

Cream and butter

Once more of a treat than an everyday ingredient, cream and butter are both by-products of the natural butterfat contained in milk. Cream nowadays is produced by using a centrifuge to separate it from the milk. Once, however, it was made by the startlingly simple process of setting fresh milk to one side and allowing the cream to rise to the surface, then skimming it off. Making it in this way is virtually impossible today, as most milk sold commercially is homogenised – which means it has been treated in order to break down and disperse the fat globules evenly through the milk. This can make the milk look whiter and taste creamier. Legally, any milk not sold direct by the farmer to the end user has to be pasteurised – which means heat treated to kill off any bacteria that may be lurking in the milk.

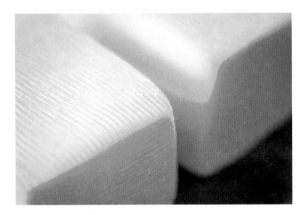

Above: Shaping butter the traditional way using butter pats

Butter is made from cream, which is beaten until the butterfat present in the cream separates from the buttermilk. Both Britain and America favour what is termed 'sweet cream butter', which means it is made with fresh cream. In continental Europe, they favour 'cultured cream butter' (also called lactic butter), where the cream is mixed with lactic acid bacteria and allowed to 'ripen' (i.e. sour very slightly) before being churned into butter, resulting in a more subtle flavour than sweet butter. While most butter is made from cow's milk, it can also be made from the milk of goats, sheep or water buffalo, with or without added salt. The keeping qualities of butter can be extended considerably by clarifying it – that is by melting and simmering it very gently to cook off all the water, then straining off through muslin to get rid of any impurities and remaining milk solids. The resulting golden liquid is clarified butter (known as ghee in India), which is valued by cooks for its rich, buttery flavour and the fact that it has a higher smoking point than ordinary butter when used as a cooking fat.

Buttermilk

Buttermilk was traditionally a by-product of the butter-making process: the white milky liquid created when cream is turned into butter. Nowadays, most commercially sold buttermilk is made by adding a fermenting culture to milk, in the same

Meet the Producer: Ivy House Dairy Farm

A herd of 230 doe-eyed Jersey cattle are at the heart of Ivy House Dairy Farm, Geoff and Kim Bowles' organic farm. Jersey cattle are noted for the higher than average butterfat content of their milk, which gives its characteristic deep yellow colour and rich creamy flavour. The Bowles sell the milk from their herd both simply as milk (from skimmed through to full fat) and also use it to make their own cream, clotted cream and buttermilk. Although the Bowles do pasteurise their milk, they don't homogenise it as is more or less standard these days, so the cream will rise to the top to form an enticing layer.

The son of a dairy farmer, Geoff Bowles 'fell in love' with Jersey cattle and decided to set up a farm with a Jersey herd. 'To my mind, they're the only pure dairy breed,' explains Geoff. 'The calves are like deer; there's no meat on them. Dairy is what they're for.' The golden colour of the milk from the high butterfat content 'comes as a surprise to people now' because they're used to the pale milk that comes from Friesians, a dual-purpose breed used for milk and for beef. 'Jersey cattle are lovely to work with,' declares Geoff. 'The cows have the nicest temperament, though the bulls have very bad tempers so you have to be careful.'

The butter-making came about one January when, due to the seasonal nature of cream sales, they found themselves with an excess of cream and decided to use it to make their own butter in the traditional way. This small-scale production is carried out by hand, a much gentler process than mechanised butter-making. 'Whereas mechanised butter is created through the use of sheer force, with the butter extruded from the machine, ours is worked by hand to force out the moisture, patted out by hand and wrapped by hand,' explains Geoff. 'The biggest demand for our butter comes from catering; pastry chefs love working with it. Not only does it have a lot of flavour, because we make it by hand, it seems to have a great elasticity that mass-produced butter lacks.'

way as for making yoghurt, then breaking down the resulting set curds to create a thick, smooth liquid with a sour tang. Buttermilk is prized in baking because it adds flavour and tenderness to baked goods such as scones and soda bread and hotcakes or griddle cakes.

As with all dairy-making, hygienic conditions are vital when making your own buttermilk, so sterilise the cheesecloth used to strain the curd by boiling it for ten minutes before use, and pour boiling water over the utensils you will use.

Right: Cream being prepared at Ivy House Dairy for sale at the farmer's market

Yoghurt

The addition of lactic acid bacteria to milk is key to a number of fermented milk products that are created by encouraging these microbes to multiply. As they grow, they release lactic acid into the milk, creating a sour flavour that is so characteristic. Yoghurt, the most widely known of these fermented products, was made for thousands of years in many parts of the world, including Central Asia and India, but was not introduced to Western Europe until the early part of the twentieth century. Other fermented milk products include soured cream, crème fraîche and buttermilk. Originally, the fermenting process occurred naturally through the presence of bacteria in the milk, but nowadays commercial producers create them in carefully controlled conditions by adding particular strains of bacteria.

Yoghurt is made by first heating the milk, then cooling it, in order to allow the fermentation process to begin. This is triggered by adding the bacteria, usually in the form of 'live' yoghurt. (The description 'live' yoghurt refers to the fact that it has been made with a live bacterial culture and still contains these benign bacteria. The belief that certain bacteria found in yoghurt aid digestion is leading to manufacturers adding 'probiotic' bacteria – that is bacteria that are beneficial to health – to yoghurt.) The milk is then left to incubate at the correct temperature to allow the bacteria to thrive and turn the milk into set yoghurt. A general rule of thumb is that the longer the yoghurt incubates, the firmer and more acid it becomes. Straining yoghurt through fine muslin to remove the whey is the traditional way to thicken its texture, with Greek yoghurt being an example of this. The longer the yoghurt is strained for, the thicker it is, becoming, in effect, a soft cheese, such as the Middle Eastern labne.

Left: Yoghurt is a popular healthy option for breakfast or dessert due to the 'helpful' bacteria present in it

Meet the producer: Neal's Yard Creamery

Working in his small Herefordshire dairy, Charlie carefully makes a small range of subtly flavourful dairy products using both goat's milk, from which he makes three cheeses, and cow's milk, from which he makes one cheese, yoghurt and crème fraîche.

'I'm making different styles of small cheeses,' he explains, 'the sorts of cheeses a farmer in France with some goats might make.' The start of his working day sees Charlie collecting the milk he uses from two local farms, who have supplied him with 'lovely milk' for many years, arriving back home with the milk 'in time for breakfast'. For his cheeses, Charlie uses a traditional kid rennet from France, which he finds 'gives the best flavour' and produces 'nice, silky' curds.

The first cheese that Charlie made commercially is Perroche, a French-inspired fresh goat's cheese, which he continues to produce to this day. Making Perroche requires 'very gentle handling' as goat's milk makes very fragile curds. The milk is left to coagulate overnight, then the curd is cut into cubes with a steel ruler in the bucket and carefully transferred into plastic moulds. 'It's very delicate curd, so if I drop a cube just six inches onto the surface, it breaks.' The curd is left to self-drain in the mould for an hour, then filled up again and left to drain overnight. The following day the cheeses are brined in a brine solution for 12 minutes. 'This firms up the cheese,' explains Charlie, 'and adds salt for flavour and for keeping.' The dainty cheeses are then sold just plain or coated with rosemary, tarragon or dill.

In addition to his cheeses, Neal's Yard Creamery is noted for its yoghurt and crème fraîche. 'To make these I need to create a receptive growing medium for the cultures that I add,' explains Charlie. First, the milks are enriched with a little cream (for the yoghurt) and pure double cream (for the crème

fraîche) and are heated to pasteurisation point to eliminate other bacteria. The yoghurt milk is then cooled to 45°C (113°F) and the crème fraîche to 25°C (77°F), temperatures at which the cultures will thrive. While still liquid, the warm milk and cream are poured into pots and incubated until they thicken and set, the yoghurt for 3 to 4 hours and the crème fraîche for 16 hours at a cooler temperature. Both the quality of the locally sourced milk and the starter cultures he uses 'add a depth of flavour' to both his yoghurt and his crème fraîche, which, in his words, have 'a long, rich flavour and longer rounder finish, not just a simple acidic kick'.

Sourcing the ingredients

Using good-quality milk is essential, with several artisanal cheese makers choosing to work with unpasteurised or 'raw' milk rather than pasteurised milk, valuing its flavour. Raw milk for domestic use is rather hard to track down, but can be found at farm shops or markets (see page 16).

Virtually all commercially available milks have been pasteurised and usually homogenised (see page 12). Pasteurised milk and cream can be used for making butter, cheese and yoghurt, but ultra-heat treatment (UHT) milk, where the milk is very briefly heated to 129–149°C (265–300°F), is not suitable for cheese making because the process affects the nature of the proteins within the milk.

Cow's milk is by far the most widely available. The revival of artisanal cheese making also means that there is renewed interest in reviving traditional breeds of dairy cows noted for the quality and flavour of their milk, such as Ayrshires in Britain or Brown Swiss cows in the United States. The milk from Jersey cows contains 5.2% fat (as opposed to the 3.6% fat found in Holstein Friesians) and is a deep yellow colour with a rich, creamy flavour. The milk is much valued for cream and butter making, but the size of the fat globules makes it difficult for producing cheese. Cow's milk is sold in a range of fat contents, from skimmed to full fat, allowing for experimentation when it comes to making dairy products at home.

Many people with a lactic intolerance prefer dairy products made from sheep's milk or goat's milk, as their fat globules are not only far smaller, but are also more evenly dispersed (i.e. naturally homogenised), making them more digestible.

Bright white sheep's milk has a high fat and protein content, which results in a particularly nutritious cheese. The milk has a distinctive nutty flavour, which also often characterises the resulting cheese and yoghurt. Goat's milk, also bright white, has a subtle but distinctive flavour. Buffalo milk, rarely offered on sale to the public, is a brilliant white milk highly valued by cheese makers because its high fat and protein content allow for a very good yield of cheese from the milk. The most famous cheese made from buffalo milk is mozzarella.

How to store

Keeping your homemade dairy products cool is essential. Butter, soft cheeses and yoghurt should all be stored in the refrigerator, either in containers or well wrapped to prevent them becoming tainted by other foods. Butter will keep for several weeks, although it can be frozen for up to 8 months; soft cheeses for 1–2 weeks, and yoghurt for 2 weeks.

Left: A Jersey cow
Right: Full-fat cow's milk to be used in the yoghurt recipe on page 22

Making yoghurt

This recipe uses full-fat cow's milk, but you can use other milks such as lower-fat cow's, goat's or sheep's. In order to trigger the fermentation process, you need to add 'live' yoghurt, which will be labelled as such on the pot and is available in chiller cabinets. The yoghurt needs to be incubated in a warm spot, such as an insulated cooler box in which you place a couple of sealed jars of freshly boiled water in order to raise the temperature.

800ml full-fat milk

3 tablespoons 'live' yoghurt

Equipment needed

cheese-making thermometer

large sterilised jar or
small sterilised jars

Makes 600ml

1 Assemble all the ingredients and equipment.

2 Place the milk in a heavy-based pan. Heat the milk gently until it reaches 85°C (185°F), checking it with the thermometer. Remove from direct heat and allow to cool for 10–15 minutes until the temperature reduces to 43°C (110°F). Now mix the 'live' yoghurt into the warm milk.

3 Carefully pour the mixture into a sterilised jar or jars. Cover and set aside to incubate in a warm place for 7–8 hours until set to your taste. Store in the refrigerator for up to a week. This is delicious served with honey (see main picture).

Making cream cheese

The simplest way to start making cheese at home is with soft cheese, by draining yoghurt through cheesecloth. Alternatively, you can curdle warm milk using lemon juice or rennet, then drain the curds in muslin or cheesecloth to create a soft cheese. Should you be bitten by the cheese-making bug, then it's worth buying a few pieces of equipment, such as a cheese-making thermometer and some muslin for draining and also some cheese-making rennet. Thanks to the internet, it's now very easy to track down specialist mail-order cheese-making companies to supply you. Many of these also offer starter packets of bacterial cultures to help you create specific cheeses, such as curd cheese or mozzarella. As its name suggests, the soft cheese we are making here is made from milk enriched with cream.

600ml full-fat milk

400ml double cream

100ml 'live' yoghurt

5 drops of cheese-making rennet, dissolved in a little water that has been boiled and cooled

salt

Equipment needed

cheese-making thermometer

colander

large square of muslin or cheesecloth

Makes 200g–300g, depending on how long it drains for (200g being after overnight draining)

1 Mix together the milk, double cream and yoghurt in a large, heavy-based pan. Gently heat this mixture until it reaches 38°C (100°F), testing with the thermometer. Remove from direct heat and stir in the rennet mixture. Stir for 2–3 minutes, during which time the milk mixture will begin to curdle. Cover and set aside to stand for 1 hour until the curd has set.

2 Using a shallow, slotted spoon, cut through the mixture, right down to the bottom of the pan, at roughly 2.5cm intervals in both directions. This helps the curds to separate from the whey, allowing more liquid to stay in the pan when you transfer the curds to the muslin (see step 4). Leave to stand for a further 20 minutes.

3 Using the same spoon, carefully remove the curds from the pan, allowing the whey to drain back into the pan.

4 Put the curds into a muslin-lined colander standing on a deep plate. Gather up the muslin and squeeze the curds to encourage the whey to drain off through the muslin. (The curds need to drain for at least 8 hours, so you will need to tie the muslin up and suspend it over the colander; a longer drainage produces a denser-textured cheese.)

5 Season the cream cheese with salt, adding only a little at a time and mixing thoroughly. Store covered in the refrigerator for up to 2 weeks.

Making butter

Making your own butter is very easy and requires no specialist equipment (though if you can get hold of butter bats, you will be able to form the butter into the traditional blocks). Unsalted butter keeps for only a few days, but adding salt prolongs its life, allowing butter to be kept for a couple of weeks, covered, in the fridge.

300ml whipping or double cream, at room temperature

100ml very cold water

salt

Equipment needed

food processor fitted with metal cutting blades

sieve

potato masher

Makes 130g

1 Place the cream in the food processor and blend for a few minutes until the cream separates into pale yellow butter and a milky-white liquid, which is the buttermilk. Using the sieve, drain off the buttermilk, reserving this for drinking or for using in cooking. You need to now remove any buttermilk remaining in the butter as otherwise it will turn rancid and taint the butter.

2 Return the butter to the food processor and add the cold water. Blend, then drain off the cloudy liquid. Repeat this process four times, until the liquid running off is practically clear.

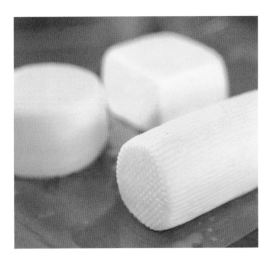

3 Transfer the butter to a large bowl and work by mashing with a masher to bring the butter together and to press out any remaining water, draining it off as it comes out. Season the butter with salt to taste and work with the masher until the butter is smooth and firm, with no more water coming out when worked.

4 Transfer the butter to a ramekin or a mould or simply shape with a spoon. Cut into pats to serve. To store the butter, wrap in waxed paper to prevent it being tainted by smells from other foods. Keep in the refrigerator.

Making buttermilk

Buttermilk was historically a by-product of making butter — the white, milky liquid created when cream is turned into butter. Nowadays, however, most commercially produced buttermilk is made by adding a culture to milk to ferment it, then stirring the resulting curd to make a thick, smooth liquid with a sour tang. A quick and simple way of making buttermilk at home is to sour milk by adding vinegar or lemon juice.

500ml full-fat milk, at room temperature

2 tablespoons lemon juice or white wine vinegar

Makes 500ml buttermilk

1 Assemble the ingredients.

2 Place the room-temperature milk in a bowl. Add in the lemon juice or white wine vinegar.

3 Stir to mix well together. Leave to stand for 15 minutes, during which time the milk will thicken slightly and take on a faintly sour tang. Store covered in the refrigerator where it will keep for up to a week and stir before serving.

Using your produce

Cream of cauliflower soup

This is a particularly creamy soup adapted from a French recipe. Originally, it was thickened by beating in egg yolks, but I have found that the buttermilk gives it a lighter touch. Do make sure that you use a firm, fresh cauliflower as once they go soft, cauliflowers tend to turn slightly bitter and so ruin the flavour of the soup.

I large firm cauliflower

750ml stock (chicken or vegetable)

pinch of nutmeg

salt, to taste

300ml buttermilk (see page 28)

Serves 4–6

1 Clean the cauliflower, remove the outer leaves and break up into small pieces or florets. Cook these in lightly salted boiling water until soft. Drain and add the cooking water to the stock.

2 Pound the cauliflower to a purée and return it to the saucepan. Pour in the stock, add a pinch of nutmeg, and extra salt if necessary. Simmer for about 15 minutes and then remove from the heat.

3 Allow it to cool and then pour in the buttermilk, beating vigorously with a balloon whisk. Gently re-heat, taking great care that the soup does not boil and so curdle the buttermilk.

Beef in buttermilk

The Austrians have a particular method of dealing with poor-quality beef. They marinate it in buttermilk sharpened with capers and lemon rind and then bake it slowly in a clay pot.

300ml buttermilk (see page 28)

2 medium onions, finely chopped

I teaspoon capers

I garlic clove

grated rind of I lemon

I½–2kg beef (any cheap cut)

salt and pepper, to taste

Equipment needed

clay pot

Serves 4–6

1 Preheat the oven to 200°C/400°F/Gas 6. Prepare the clay pot by soaking it in water for 15 minutes.

2 Mix the buttermilk with onion, capers, garlic and lemon rind and pour over the beef. Leave the meat to soak up the flavour for a minimum of four hours, turning it occasionally in the marinade.

3 Put the beef and marinade into the prepared clay pot. Cover and bake for two hours. Remove the lid and allow the meat to brown and cook for a further 20 minutes.

4 When cooked, carve the meat into thin slices and arrange on a dish. Strain the onion and liquidise with the capers to form a purée. Skim the gravy to remove the fat and reduce to half the quantity. Stir into the purée and pour over the sliced meat.

Beetroot, goats' cheese and pine nut salad with melba toast

This salad has a wintry, festive sumptuousness, thanks to the deep red of the beetroot and the bright white of the homemade cheese.

750g small, unpeeled beetroot, trimmed

12 slices white bread

500g mixed leaves

200g crumbly goats' cheese

100g pine nuts, toasted in a dry frying pan

bunch of basil

2 garlic cloves, chopped

5 tablespoons olive oil

freshly squeezed juice of 2 lemons

sea salt and freshly ground black pepper

Serves 12

1 Preheat the oven to 180°C/350°F/Gas 4. Put the beetroot into a roasting tin and roast in the oven for 45 minutes. Remove from the oven, leave to cool, then peel and quarter.

2 Meanwhile, to make the melba toast, toast the slices of bread, then remove the crusts. Using a large, sharp knife, split each piece of toast through the middle, to give two whole slices of toast with one soft bread side each. Cut in half diagonally, then cook under a preheated grill, soft side up, until golden and curled. Watch the toasts carefully, as they can burn quickly.

3 Put the mixed leaves onto a big serving dish, add the beetroot, crumble the goats' cheese on top, then sprinkle with pine nuts and torn basil leaves.

4 Put the garlic, oil and lemon juice into a small bowl or jar. Add salt and pepper, mix well, then pour over the salad. Serve with the melba toast.

Baked bream

Low-fat yoghurt has a tendency to curdle when boiled or baked, so, if using, it is advisable to stabilise it before cooking. To save time, you can stabilise a large amount and keep in the fridge for a week or so.

To stabilise the yoghurt, if necessary
500ml low-fat yoghurt (see page 22)
1 egg white, lightly beaten
pinch of salt

1 bream, 750g–1kg, cleaned, gutted and descaled
1 teaspoon coriander seeds
2 cloves garlic
6 peppercorns
1 teaspoon salt crystals
1 onion, finely chopped
grated rind and juice of 1 lemon

Equipment needed
fish brick or terracotta oven pot

Serves 4

1 Beat the yoghurt in a saucepan and stir in the egg white and pinch of salt. Gently bring to the boil, stirring constantly, with a regular action and then simmer for about 10 minutes on a very low heat as the yoghurt must not be allowed to burn. The yoghurt will form a smooth thick paste, which can be added to meat or vegetables and reheated without fear of curdling or separating.

2 Prepare the fish brick or terracotta oven pot by soaking it in water for 15 minutes.

3 Crush the coriander seeds and garlic with the peppercorns and salt crystals and mix the paste with the onion and lemon rind.

4 Lay the fish in the prepared fish brick or pot and spread the mixture all over the fish. Pour over the lemon juice. Place the brick in a cool oven and bake for an hour at 180°C/350°F/Gas 4.

5 When the fish is cooked, lift it on to a serving dish and keep warm. Pour the juice into the yoghurt. Stir vigorously. Heat gently until almost boiling. Pour over the fish and serve immediately.

Wild mushroom and butter bean soup

Believe it or not, this soup is best made with dried wild mushrooms. To dry your mushrooms, just cut them into slices, spread them out on to a wire rack and leave them in the oven on the lowest possible setting for at least 6 hours. But if you are not the hunter/gatherer type who has picked their own, simply buy a packet.

25g dried wild mushrooms
2 tablespoons olive oil
1 onion, sliced
2 garlic cloves, crushed
500g butter beans, soaked overnight in water
150ml full-fat yoghurt (see page 22)
sea salt and freshly ground black pepper
25g butter (see page 26)
parsley, chopped (optional)

Equipment needed:
muslin-lined sieve
hand blender or food processor

Serves 4–6

1 Put the mushrooms in a suitable bowl, pour over about 300ml boiling water and leave to soak for about 30 minutes or until the mushrooms are quite soft. Using a slotted spoon, lift out the mushrooms and refresh them by putting them in a clean bowl with just enough cold water to cover. Reserve the water in which the mushrooms have been soaking, but if it looks particularly gritty strain it through a muslin-lined sieve. Otherwise, just leave it as a few particles will not do any harm – actually, they will probably increase the flavour of the soup.

2 In a large saucepan heat the olive oil, add the onion and garlic and cook gently over a moderate heat to soften for about 5–7 minutes. Drain the butter beans and add to the saucepan, stirring with a wooden spoon until they are well coated with the olive oil. Then pour in 700ml water and the water in which the mushrooms have been soaking, gently bring to the boil and simmer for about 90 minutes or until the butter beans are completely softened.

3 Using either a hand blender or food processor, whiz the soup until it is smooth. Return to the pan, stir in the yoghurt, adjust the seasoning and gently reheat. If you like your soup with a bit of texture, keep a few whole butter beans back before you purée the soup, then stir them in with the yoghurt.

4 Meanwhile, melt the butter in a suitable sauté pan. Squeeze the mushrooms with your hands until they are dry and roughly chop them into small pieces. Add the mushrooms to the pan and sauté gently over a medium heat for 5 minutes or until they are tender. Stir the mushrooms into the soup, adjust the seasoning and, if you think the soup needs a little colour, sprinkle over some chopped parsley just before serving.

Buttermilk cornbread

Stoneground yellow cornmeal gives this cornbread a wonderful texture, and the buttermilk and honey make for a soft, sweet crumb. For a change, you could add 3 tablespoons toasted pine nuts, fresh or frozen corn kernels or grated mature cheese.

140g fine yellow cornmeal, preferably stoneground

125g plain flour

1½ teaspoons baking powder

½ teaspoon bicarbonate of soda

½ teaspoon sea salt

1 large egg

50g unsalted butter, melted

3 tablespoons honey

225ml buttermilk (see page 28)

Equipment needed:

20cm square cake tin, well greased

Makes 1 medium loaf (6–8 portions)

1 Preheat the oven to 200°C/400°F/Gas 6.

2 Put the cornmeal, flour, baking powder, bicarbonate of soda and salt in a large bowl and stir with a wooden spoon until the ingredients are thoroughly mixed.

3 In a separate bowl, beat the egg with the melted butter, honey and buttermilk. Stir into the dry ingredients to make a thick, smooth batter.

4 Transfer the mixture to the prepared tin and spread evenly.

5 Bake for 15–20 minutes until golden and a cocktail stick inserted into the centre comes out clean. Turn out onto a bread board, cut into large squares and serve warm.

6 Best eaten the same day. Can be frozen for up to a month – gently warm before serving.

Summer berry frozen yoghurt

Use full-fat homemade yoghurt for this recipe and you will be rewarded with a delectable dessert. Low-fat yoghurt can give an unpleasant, icy texture.

500g mixed summer berries, such as strawberries, blackberries and raspberries
150g caster sugar
500g full-fat yoghurt (see page 22)

Equipment needed:
food processor
fine-meshed nylon sieve
an ice cream machine (optional)

Serves 4

1 Warm the berries and sugar in a saucepan over low heat for several minutes, until the fruit begins to release its juices. Transfer to a food processor and blend to a purée. Push the purée through a fine-meshed nylon sieve to remove the seeds. Stir in the yoghurt.

2 Churn in an ice cream machine until almost frozen. Transfer to a freezerproof container and freeze until ready to serve.

3 You can also make the frozen yoghurt without a machine. The mixture should be frozen in a shallow container. When almost solid, beat it well with a wire whisk or electric beater until smooth, then return to the freezer. Repeat the process twice more, to break down the ice crystals, and the result will be smooth and silky.

4 Transfer the frozen yoghurt to the fridge for 20–30 minutes before serving, to let it soften evenly throughout.

5 Homemade frozen yoghurt is best eaten as soon as possible after being made, and certainly within a week.

Thin crackers

These crackers bear absolutely no relation to shop-bought cream crackers as they are far crispier and have a far more interesting taste. These biscuits have a short-life and should really be eaten on the day they are made. If you do want to keep them, put them in a tin while still warm along with a sheet of greaseproof paper to prevent them from going soggy. You can always revive them by warming them briefly in the oven.

225g strong white flour
large pinch of salt
I teaspoon baking powder
55g butter (see page 26), cut into small pieces
6 tablespoons single cream
ground sea salt, for sprinkling

Makes 15–20

1 Preheat the oven to 180°C/350°F/Gas 4. Generously grease a baking sheet with butter.

2 Sift the flour into a bowl with the salt and baking powder. Add the butter and cut it into the flour with a knife. Then rub it in lightly with the fingertips, until it is the texture of fine breadcrumbs. Stir in the cream, then gather the mixture together to make a firm dough, adding a tablespoon of water if necessary.

3 On a lightly floured flat surface, roll the dough out very thinly, pressing down quite hard on it. Using a 7.5cm biscuit cutter, cut into rounds. Arrange the biscuits on the prepared baking sheet, prick them all over with a fork and sprinkle over a little sea salt. Bake in the preheated oven for 10–15 minutes, or until golden brown. Turn out on wire racks and leave to cool.

Fruit kebabs

You can use slices of any firm fruit — apples, pineapples or plums — or strawberries or blackberries for a fruit kebab. And you can vary the flavour of the butter by using a different alcohol, such as brandy, whisky or gin, or by adding a handful of freshly chopped mint or a pinch of chopped almonds or walnuts.

I punnet strawberries
4 large apricots, cut into thick wedges
50g unsalted butter (see page 26)
I tablespoon brown sugar
I tablespoon rum

Serves 4

1 Preheat the grill.

2 Thread the fruit on four individual wooden or metal skewers, alternating the strawberries with the apricot wedges. If the berries are very large, cut them in half, but do not bother to hull them.

3 Whiz the butter with the brown sugar in a blender and, with the machine still running, pour in the rum. Using a pastry brush, paint the fruit all over with the flavoured butter. Grill for about a minute on each side or for just long enough to melt the butter and heat the fruit.

Tip: If you need to wash the strawberries, do so with a little red or white wine rather than water. It will help the fruit stay firm and enhance the flavour.

Chapter 2

THE BAKERY

The foods we make from flour and bake in the oven play a very significant part in our lives. Bread is one of the most fundamental of our foods, an everyday staple with a symbolic and spiritual resonance. You only have to think of the Christian prayer, 'Give us this day our daily bread' or the expression 'breaking bread' to realise it holds a special place in our lives. Flour, enriched with fat and eggs and sweetened with sugar, is also the base of treats such as biscuits, cakes and pastries. Baking a cake is still the way in which we mark our special occasions — birthdays, weddings, Easter and Christmas.

There is something about baking at home and the process by which a few basic ingredients – flour, a raising agent such as yeast or baking powder, water, fat or oil, and sugar – are transformed into breads, pastries, cakes and biscuits, that is profoundly satisfying.

Bread

The history of bread dates back to prehistoric times, when flatbreads made from a paste of crushed grains mixed with water were cooked on stones or embers. The story of bread is inevitably closely tied to the very early days of human agriculture and the cultivation of grains, including wheat, which first took place in Western Asia before 7000 BCE.

Grinding the grain to make flour for bread was a long and labour-intensive process. It began with the use of grinding stones, known as saddle stones, and led to the invention of the windmill and watermill, which powered huge millstones to grind the grain. The nineteenth-century roller mill, where multiple steel rollers ground the grain, allowed white flour to be produced quickly and efficiently and sold cheaply. Since Roman times, bread made from white flour had been an exclusive food, the preserve of the wealthy, but the new roller mills and mechanisation put an end to that. Today,

the majority of flours are produced through roller milling, with only a handful of craft millers using traditional grinding stones to produce their flour.

It was during the twentieth century that baking underwent a major change, moving from the traditional methods used by small bakeries towards industrialised ones. The slow rising of dough was replaced by processes using accelerated dough development, which called for the addition of chemical 'improvers', preservatives, emulsifiers and a speeded-up process of intense mechanical agitation. Most bread is still produced in this way, although in many countries craft bakers are still able to practise their craft and serve a niche market.

Pastry

Flour is the base for not only bread, but also pastry, cakes and biscuits. Making pastry from the mixture of flour, fat and liquid is usually thought of as a separate craft from baking bread. There are many types of pastry, from fine filo pastry, which comes from Greece and the eastern Mediterranean and is used in layered pastries such as sweet baklava, to egg-rich choux pastry, used by the French in creations such as éclairs, religieuses and croquembouche, and buttery flaky pastry, used for croissants. Pastry's first use remains as a case for other ingredients – an apple pie, mushroom vol-au-vent or a Cornish pasty with its crimped edge forming a 'handle' to hold the pasty by, so dirty hands didn't touch the filling. In medieval times, such pastry cases were called 'coffers'.

Left: The trademark slits on a French baguette help the escape of steam and carbon dioxide
Right: A bakery will tend not to supply just one type of product but will be able to provide the customer with a range of both sweet and savoury items

Flour

All good bakers stress the importance of using good-quality flour and, more importantly, the right flour for the job. Most flour is made from wheat, which is valued above other grains for its high gluten content: gluten molecules stretch and hold their shape, so the breads rise successfully. Nowadays, the most widely grown species of wheat for bread making is *Triticum aestivum*. It has several cultivars, and those with a high gluten content are known as 'hard' wheats which produce 'strong' flour.

Flours are also made from other grains, such as maize, buckwheat, barley or rye, and there is a renewed interest in ancient grains, such as spelt or kamut, and flours made from these grains are increasingly available to the home baker. There are also flours made from nuts, such as chestnuts, and pulses, such as gram flour from chickpeas.

To make a leavened bread – one that rises – you need flour with a high gluten content, often called 'strong', but when making pastries or cakes, less gluten is needed as you want a softer, yielding texture.

Below: Freshly milled flour
Opposite: Use the heel of your hands when kneading

Grades of wheat flour

Bran The hard outer layer of a cereal grain that is removed during the milling process.

Brown flour Usually contains around 85 per cent of the original bran and wheat germ.

Granary flour A brown flour that has been combined with malted wheat grains to give a nutty flavour.

Self-raising flour A low-protein white flour that has had a raising agent, such as baking powder, added to it.

Soft flour Very finely milled white flour with a low gluten content, used to give cakes a higher rise and finer texture.

Stoneground flour Flour that has been milled in a traditional way by grinding the grain with millstones rather than metal rollers (see page 38), which means that the elements of the grain – the bran, wheat germ and endosperm – are crushed together.

Strong flour This is flour with a high protein content, ideal for breadmaking; it comes in many different forms, such as white, wholemeal, mixed grain and granary.

Wheat germ This forms part of the wheat kernel and provides nourishment for the seed.

Wheat germ flour White or brown flour that has at least 10 per cent added wheat germ.

White flour Flour that has been milled and sieved to extract the bran and wheat germ, giving it a low protein content.

Wholemeal flour As its name suggests, this flour is made by grinding up whole wheat kernels – the bran, wheat germ and endosperm – with nothing removed.

Meet the producer: Staff of Life

A love of baking ever since he was a boy saw Simon Thomas, together with his wife Julie, set up Staff of Life bakery in 1997, producing a range of hand-made breads and cakes from locally produced flour.

'Ingredients are key to my baking,' states Simon. 'In flour I look for a combination of flavour and gluten protein, choosing the flour according to the bread we want to make. So for our classic wholemeal, I use a mix of Salkeld Watermill flour, which is very flavourful and coarse, together with flour from Carr's Mills, who make very consistent flour, for strength. Our bread is ultra-low in salt, under one per cent of sea salt, so that rather than just tasting salt, the taste of the grain itself comes through. Our spelt loaf, for example, has a deep caramel flavour to it that comes from the spelt.'

To raise his breads, Simon uses Fermipan dried yeast and, intriguingly, a home-made elderflower-based sourdough starter, carrying over some of the dough each time he makes sourdough to use it to start the next batch. 'There's a natural yeast in elderflowers, which is far stronger than baker's yeast and works beautifully,' he explains. 'Because it's so strong, we use a low ratio of starter to flour, 10 per cent rather than the normal 20 per cent, which makes our sourdough less sour. Lots of the people who buy it normally don't like sourdough.'

Having made the dough, Simon allows for a long, slow, gentle first rising, followed by shorter second and sometimes even a third rising. 'Our bread is made very slowly. Our doughs all rise for a minimum of 15 hours and a lot of them have two days' rising. The time gives a lot of flavour and makes the dough easy to handle. It's a soft dough, so you don't have to punch at it, instead you knead it gently; persuasion rather than confrontation.' The bread is baked in a

professional electric oven. 'Each batch bakes differently so I keep a close eye on it. It gets so I can tell when it's ready by the smell.'

Of the bread-making process, Simon observes, 'It's a bit like training animals: every dough has its own character. Some mornings you can touch the dough and know that it's going to make fantastic bread today. Making bread is an easily acquired skill. I run bread-making courses, and there's an expression people get on their faces when they've got it; the same expression that someone gets when they realise how simple a magic trick really is.'

Yeast and other raising agents

In order for bread to rise, it needs to have a raising agent added to the dough, with yeast the best known of these agents. Given the right conditions, yeast works within the dough by multiplying and creating bubbles of carbon dioxide, so causing it to rise. One yeast species in particular, *Saccharomyces cerevisiae*, which is widely used in baking, is valued for its reliability as a raising agent and its lack of a pronounced flavour, therefore allowing the character of the flour to shine through. It is this yeast that is available commercially in a number of forms: fresh, dried (active dry) and easy-blend (instant dry).

Fresh yeast, also known as cake or compressed yeast, is sold in the form of a soft, moist cake which crumbles easily. Many craft bakers will only use fresh yeast, feeling that it gives a slower rise and creates bread with a better crumb and flavour. Dried yeast, which comes in granular form, is a dormant form, requiring immersion in warm water to activate it before being added to the dough. Easy-blend yeast, also in granular form, does not require a separate immersion in warm water to activate it and can simply be sprinkled dry directly into the flour. It is made from a very fast-acting strain of *Saccharomyces cerevisiae*, so grows very vigorously, quickly creating carbon dioxide.

Whilst fresh yeast can be tricky to source, dried and easy-blend are widely available. Because of their concentrated nature, dried yeasts are more powerful than fresh yeast and so less is needed to raise the dough. If substituting yeasts, a general rule of thumb is to substitute half the amount of dried yeast for the amount of fresh yeast and a quarter of the amount of easy-blend yeast for the amount of fresh yeast.

Wild yeasts are naturally present in the atmosphere and the aim is to capture and harness them to make 'proper' sourdough – see page 54. Using a commercially produced *Saccharomyces cerevisiae* yeast for a sourdough starter does not work because the process of making sourdough requires wild yeasts, often from the genus *Candida*, to dominate. Once created, a portion of this sourdough, rich in wild yeasts, is mixed into the dough to cause it to rise. Sourdough starters need to be looked after and 'fed' to keep them active and are perpetuated by keeping back a portion to use for the next batch of the dough. Many craft bakers have carefully nurtured sourdough starters that have survived for several years. Although a sour tang is a characteristic flavour of bread made using sourdough, because populations of wild yeasts vary from place to place, sourdoughs range in flavour according to region, with, for example, a San Francisco sourdough loaf tasting different from a French *pain au levain*. Another characteristic of using a sourdough starter is that the dough will take longer to rise than one made from commercial yeast.

Creating the right environment for all yeasts to grow in is important, with yeast needing moisture, food and warmth. When making bread, liquid (usually just water) is added to the flour to create the dough. Flours vary in their ability to absorb water, so it should be added gradually. Many bakers weigh their water rather than measuring it, as they find this more accurate. Yeast's favourite food is sugar, which is why sugar is often used in bread recipes. At low temperatures, yeasts become dormant, but at higher temperatures, they can die; the optimum temperature for yeasts to grow in is around 26°C (79°F). Having made your dough with yeast and provided it with moisture and food in the form of water and sugar, you should then set it aside to rest and rise in a warm, draught-free place.

Other raising agents used in baking are chemical raisers such as bicarbonate of soda, which works when combined with acid elements such as buttermilk or a sourdough culture. Baking powder contains both bicarbonate of soda and an acid element.

Opposite: Yeast mixed with water to produce bubbles of carbon dioxide
Above right: A stack of freshly baked foccacia
Right: This loaf has been slashed multiple times to allow the dough to rise

Pastry

As a general rule, pastry is made from a mixture of flour, fat and water. There are a number of types of pastries — shortcrust, puff, choux and filo — with the differences arising from the techniques that go into making them. For shortcrust, you rub the fat into the flour with your fingertips. For puff pastry, the fat is carefully layered into the dough and rolled out.

Shortcrust pastry, classically made with a ratio of half the weight of fat to flour, then bound together with a little water or beaten egg, is widely used for both sweet and savoury baking. There are many versions of shortcrust pastries, made with differing ratios of fat to flour and different fats. Butter, for example, gives a buttery richness to the pastry, whilst lard, often used in savoury baking, is valued for the melting texture it gives to the pastry. Pastries can be sweetened or flavoured with ingredients such as cocoa, ground nuts or vanilla, making them an extremely versatile foodstuff.

Above left: Almond croissants are made from a leavened variant of puff pastry and rolled to form their distinctive crescent shape
Left: Perennial breakfast favourite, the *pain au chocolat*
Opposite: Olive and rosemary foccacia

Meet the producer: Richard Bertinet

An eloquent champion for real bread, French baker Richard Bertinet is noted not only for his range of fine breads but also for his ability to teach bread making and pastry making – an aspect of his work he finds deeply rewarding.

He has a very clear idea of how to make bread. 'To start with, you need a good dough to make good bread. I use a higher ratio of water to flour in my dough than most people, so around 500g of water to 1kg of good strong bread flour. People are scared of sticky dough; they find it messy. To me it's normal, it's not sticky. So many people add flour to the surface or sprinkle it over the dough as they work it. You don't want to do that, as you're changing the ratio of flour to water. I use a fresh yeast from France, L'Hirondelle, the same one I've used for many years. It's beautiful to use. I use as little yeast as possible. Dried yeast to me is too powerful.'

Richard's distinctive kneading method is central to how he makes bread. Rather than pushing the dough with palms and knuckles, he lifts the dough in the air, up and over on itself, then slaps it down on the surface, working the dough in this way until, after a few minutes, it becomes elastic and supple. 'There is a technique to it,' he cautions. 'It must be done carefully. It's not about bashing the dough. You don't need to be strong, but you must use your whole body. Kneading the dough the way I do adds in air,' he explains, 'and makes a light loaf. Nobody wants to make a heavy, dense loaf.'

When it comes to making pastry, a common mistake in Richard's view is rough handling. 'Overworking the pastry is very common. You need to be gentle and it's very important to let it rest enough. A bit of planning is important when it comes to pastry. Be patient; don't be scared. People come on my course very

scared of making pastry; we teach them how to make it and how to roll it and when they leave, the fear factor has gone.'

The bread oven

The Ancient Egyptians are usually credited with the invention of enclosed ovens in which to bake bread. In order to preserve precious fuel, there is a long tradition in many societies of communal baking, with the baker's oven often being used by other members of the village, too. Today, a number of artisanal bakeries continue to use traditional wood-fired ovens in which the bread is placed straight on the preheated stones of the oven floor. Bread-lovers appreciate the particular texture these ovens give to both the crust and the base of the bread.

In these days of gas and electricity, however, most domestic cooks don't have access to a wood-fired oven. While gas and electric ovens work well for baking cakes, biscuits and pastries, they are less successful when it comes to creating a good crust on loaves of bread. One useful tip to recreate the effect of a wood-fired oven is to invest in stone or ceramic baking tiles or pizza stones, which retain heat very effectively. These should be preheated in the oven, then the bread placed directly on the hot stone and baked in the oven.

Many professional bakeries also use steam in their ovens to create a moist atmosphere in order to help the bread rise successfully. Tips for the home baker to replicate this include spraying your loaf with water before you bake it; spraying the walls of the hot oven once you've placed the loaf inside; placing a metal tray with hot water in the oven; or dropping ice cubes on the floor of the oven.

Above: A wood-fired oven will maintain heat for several hours after the fire has died

Opposite: Long Crichel bakery use a traditional wood-burning oven

Meet the producer: Long Crichel

Jamie and Rose Campbell set up Long Crichel bakery in 2000 with a very clear idea of what they wanted.

'The rules we made for ourselves were our bread would be organic, made by hand, drawing on traditional techniques, and baked in a wood-burning oven,' explains Jamie. 'We were also interested in sourdough, which, given we're in Dorset, was very rare at the time. We started making our wheat sourdough using grapes from the vine growing on the house. It's all about harvesting wild yeasts, creating an environment for them to grow in. Bread is a product of fermentation.'

An eye for fine-quality ingredients is matched by attention to method. 'As a commercial bakery one has to be consistent,' points out Jamie. 'Our dough is quite wet. We have a house way of kneading, which is to knead as little as we can get away with; we don't want to overwork the dough. The more you knead, the finer your crumb is, so we'll adjust our kneading accordingly. A fine-crumbed bread will require more kneading than a country-style loaf, which has larger bubbles inside it.' Long, slow fermentation is key to the 'depth of flavour' that Jamie looks for in the bakery's breads. 'We create what's perceived to be a typical English loaf: light, with a fine crumb. To make this we use the overnight sponge method, working with a fermented dough, which rises and collapses. This gives body and flavour. We don't want something light and insipid. Another one of our signature breads is the malted five seed bread. It's a sourdough loaf made with long fermentation of around 20 hours, which has a fantastic flavour.'

The magnificent, large wood-fired oven, which burns wood thinned from the trees on the big estate around them, is central to their distinctive style. 'Even though bread, in one way, is so simple,' comments Jamie,

'there are a huge number of variations and the baking of it is one of them. Having a wood-fired oven really does make a difference. Bakers say the best way to bake bread is with heat that's falling. You make the fire in the oven, then you close it down and allow the heat to distribute evenly. It does make a difference to the quality of the crust. We add steam to the atmosphere using a water feed, which vaporises. A hot, moist atmosphere allows the bread to be elastic and soft, open up and rise more smoothly.'

Sourcing the ingredients

Talk to any baker and they will recommend finding a flour that suits the purpose. Do bear in mind that small-scale craft millers produce flours that often have a lot of flavour but can be tricky for novice bakers to use because their gluten content may vary from batch to batch. Similarly, don't be afraid to experiment with different types of yeasts, including wild yeast sourdough, to see which you enjoy using.

How to store

All flour has a limited shelf life, with wholemeal flour deteriorating faster than white because of the presence of wheat germ. Store flour in a cool dry place. Alternatively, wrap it well in plastic or place in a plastic container and freeze it for six months to a year.

When it comes to yeast, fresh yeast deteriorates easily and should be stored in the refrigerator and used quickly. Alternatively, if you buy a large amount, cut it into 25g pieces, wrap them and store them in the freezer, where they will keep for up to six months. Dried and easy-blend yeasts, though less perishable than fresh, go stale with time and become less effective. Buy them in small amounts, store in an airtight container in a cool, dry place and use them up quickly. For your own wild yeast, see page 54.

When it comes to keeping baked goods, they should be allowed to cool, then be covered and stored in a cool, dry place. In order to keep their texture for as long as possible, store biscuits in an airtight container. Bread and pastry both freeze well.

Left: Fresh yeast mixed with water, ready to be combined with flour and salt to produce dough
Right: Wooden peels are used to place bread in and out of the oven

Techniques

There are several key processes essential to good baking and pastry making. As with many culinary skills, the more you practise, the simpler it becomes.

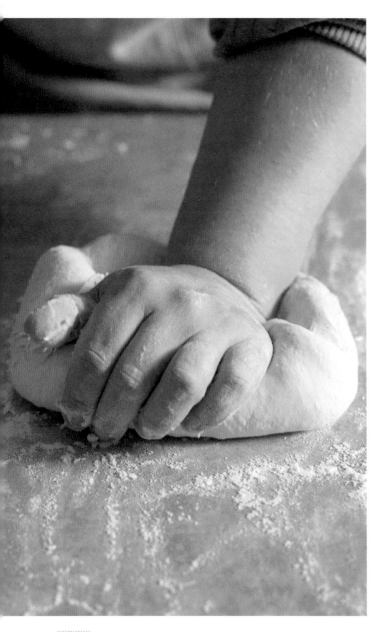

Kneading bread dough

A vital part of making bread is kneading: the process by which the dough is worked in order to develop the gluten inside the flour, making it elastic enough to rise successfully. There are many different schools of thought on how to knead, with some craft bakers advocating stretching and pushing the dough on a work surface, while others (see page 45) advocate lifting up the dough and folding it over on itself. A dough-scraper, to gather together the dough and clean it off your hands, is a useful piece of equipment.

Whichever kneading method you choose, experienced bakers agree that starting with a soft dough, rather than a firm, dry one, is best. Use a warm surface to knead on, such as a wooden table, as a cold surface like marble will make the dough too cool. Avoid adding extra flour to the work surface or your dough, as this will simply make your bread too dry. As you work the dough, you're looking for it to change texture, taking on a smooth, pliable, elastic quality. Once the dough has been kneaded, it should be loosely covered with a damp tea towel or clingfilm and placed in a warm, draught-free spot until doubled in size. Depending on the recipe, a second or even third rising may be required. Between risings, dough should be 'knocked back' by lifting it from the bowl and kneading it for a minute or two.

Left: If dough is not kneaded for long enough it will collapse, creating a dense, unappetising bread
Right: Bakers use a lame, a double-sized cutting tool, to slash their loaves prior to putting them in the oven

Shaping bread

When it comes to shaping bread, there are a number of ways to go about it and many shapes to choose from. Proving baskets, also known as bannetons, are designed to shape the dough as it rises or 'proves'. Dough can also be set aside to rise, then shaped as desired either freeform or by using loaf tins.

Slashing the bread is done not only for decorative purposes but also to allow the dough to expand correctly. Make sure you use a very sharp knife to slash the dough.

Making pastry

When it comes to making and handling pastry, it is important to keep it cool because of its fat content. If the fat begins to melt, the pastry will be oily and difficult to handle. A slab of naturally cool marble is a traditional surface for making pastry on. One very simple way to make pastry successfully is to use a food processor, as the blade mixes the ingredients together quickly and effectively, though you should be careful not to over-process it. Once you've made your pastry, it's very important to rest it in the refrigerator, as this allows the gluten to expand, enabling it to be rolled out. Having been rested and chilled, the pastry needs to be brought back to room temperature before you roll it out, otherwise it will crack.

Making granary bread

The simplest of all breads, this loaf is made from granary flour. For extra fibre, the bread can be further enriched by adding a teaspoon of fine wheat bran and sprinkling over a little more bran before baking. Because of its high bran and wheat germ content, bread made with brown or wholemeal flour tends to have a denser texture and rises less than if made with white flour.

2 teaspoons clear honey

350ml milk

30g fresh yeast or 15g dried yeast

675g granary flour

2 teaspoons salt, plus more
for glazing

1 teaspoon bran, plus extra
for finishing

2 eggs

85g unsalted butter, melted

Makes 2 x 450g loaves

1 Put the honey with 5 tablespoons of the milk in a saucepan and heat it over a low heat until lukewarm. Remove from the heat, mix in the yeast thoroughly, then cover and leave to stand in a warm place for 15 minutes or until it bubbles. In a large bowl, sift in the flour (adding what gets left in the sieve) and salt. Add the bran, eggs and melted butter and pour in the yeast mixture with the remaining milk. Using a wooden spoon, mix until the dough comes together.

2 Knead on a flat, lightly floured surface for about 10 minutes, or until the dough is smooth. Cover with a cloth and leave to rise in a warm place until it has doubled in size.

3 Preheat the oven to 230°C/450°F/Gas 8 and lightly dust a baking tray with some flour. Knock back the dough by lifting it from the bowl and kneading it for a minute or so. Cut the dough in half and shape the pieces into two cigar-like loaves. Slash the tops with a knife. Place the loaves on the prepared baking tray, cover with a cloth and leave to prove. When they have doubled in volume, they are ready to be baked.

4 Using a pastry brush, lightly brush the loaves with a salt glaze made by dissolving a pinch of salt in 2 tablespoons of hot water. Sprinkle the tops with more bran and bake in the preheated oven for about 20–30 minutes, or until brown. Remove from the tray and leave them to cool on the wire rack.

Making a sourdough starter

The aim is to capture and grow natural or wild yeasts present in the air and flour. As they grow, they produce bubbles of carbon dioxide gas and lactic acid, which will eventually be used to leaven the dough and add flavour. For best results, use unbleached white organic flour, although rye or wholemeal flours can also be used. I recommend that you use bottled spring water, but if you use tap water it needs to be filtered, boiled and cooled first.

To begin

100g unbleached organic strong white bread flour

115ml tepid water (see recipe introduction above)

For each refreshment

100g unbleached organic strong white bread flour

tepid water (see recipe introduction above)

1 Put the flour and water in a small bowl and mix to a thick, sticky paste. Cover the bowl with a damp tea towel or muslin secured with an elastic band – don't cover the bowl with clingfilm. Leave it in a draught-free spot on a work surface, re-dampening the cloth as necessary.

2 After 2–4 days (depending on the conditions) the paste should have a skin and look bubbly. It should have a milky scent. If it smells bad rather than slightly sour, or if you can see patches of mould, or if there are no signs of life, throw it away and start again. At this stage, you should give your starter its first feed or refreshment. Add another 100g flour and enough tepid water to make a soft, sticky paste-like dough. Work the dough with your hand or a wooden spoon to get plenty of air into the mixture. Cover the bowl again with a damp cloth and leave, as before, for 24 hours.

3 The starter should look very active now. Stir well then remove and discard half of it. Add another 100g flour and enough tepid water to make a dough as before. Cover and leave as before for 12 hours.

4 At this point, the sourdough starter should look very active and ready to use – to ensure there is enough to make a batch of bread and keep some for the next batch, you will need to increase the volume. You can do this by eye or by measuring – you will need about 100g flour and enough water to make a soft sticky dough as before. The dough should be bubbly again and ready to use after 6–8 hours. However, if the dough doesn't look active enough to use after its previous refreshment, you will need to halve it once more and feed it as before.

Notes: Don't worry if your starter separates into a darkish liquid layer on top of a thicker paste. Just stir it up and feed as normal, as happens if you haven't fed the starter for a while. If it smells strongly and makes your eyes water, then it is in bad shape. Reduce it to a couple of tablespoons, then add flour and water in the same proportions as before every day until the starter is bubbly and has a milky aroma.

If you don't keep a sourdough starter, use a small piece of dough, about 150g, saved from a previous batch of bread. Gradually work in enough tepid water to make a very soft dough, cover and leave for 8 hours at room temperature, then use 200g as a starter for the recipe on page 56.

5 Once you have got a starter going, it will keep forever if you look after it. Feed it regularly, every 5 days or so, even if you are not using it. Store it in a plastic container or glass jar in the refrigerator. When you want to use it, bring the starter back to room temperature, then feed it about 6 hours before starting the recipe. It should turn bubbly again.

Making Californian sourdough

There seem to be more recipes for California and San Francisco sourdough than there are bakers in the state. Before a loaf was shaped and baked, the original pioneers and settlers kept back a portion of dough to leaven the next batch. These days bakers use a range of leavens — saved dough starter, soupy sourdough leavens, fresh yeast, dried sourdough flavourings or bicarbonate of soda. The objective is a light-textured, mildly sour, well-risen white loaf. The authentic flavour comes from the foggy atmosphere and the water of the area, which are hard to reproduce, but this is a good approximation.

200g sourdough starter (see page 54)

500ml tepid water (see recipe introduction on page 54)

15g fresh yeast (see note opposite)

900g unbleached strong white bread flour

2 teaspoons sea salt

Makes 2 medium loaves

2 Mix the flour with the salt, then gradually beat into the liquid with your hand until well mixed. The dough should feel soft but not sticky: if it feels too slack, work in extra flour, 1 tablespoon at a time; if it feels hard or dry, or there are crumbs left in the bottom of the bowl, work in extra water, 1 tablespoon at a time. Turn out onto a floured work surface and knead thoroughly to make a smooth, firm, very supple dough. Return the dough to the bowl and cover with clingfilm. For the best flavour, let rise slowly in a cool room until doubled in size, about four hours, or overnight in the refrigerator.

1 Put the starter and water into a large bowl and mix with your hand to make a soupy batter. Crumble the yeast and work it into the mixture.

3 Turn out onto a lightly floured work surface and punch down to deflate. If the dough has been stored in the refrigerator, let it come back to room temperature for 1½–2 hours before continuing. Divide the dough into two equal pieces, cover with a sheet of clingfilm and leave to rest for 10 minutes. Shape each portion into a neat ball, handling the dough as little as possible. Put onto two greased baking sheets, then slide into a large plastic bag, slightly inflate and close the end. Leave to rise at normal room temperature until almost doubled in size, about 2 hours.

4 Meanwhile, preheat the oven to 220°C/425°F/Gas 7. Put a roasting tin of water into the oven to heat, as the steam created will help develop a good crust. Uncover the loaves and quickly slash the tops in a diamond pattern using a serrated knife or a razor blade. Put into the heated, steamy oven and bake for 30 minutes or until the loaves sound hollow when tapped underneath. Cool on a wire rack and eat within five days, or toast. Can be frozen for up to a month.

Note: To use easy-blend dried yeast, mix a 7g sachet with the flour and salt, then work it into the sourdough starter and water mixture.

Making focaccia

A classic, olive oil-rich Italian bread that goes well with cold cured meats or antipasti, such as the vegetables sott'olio (page 118). Experiment by adding in different flavourings such as chopped olives, sun-dried tomatoes or chopped herbs such as rosemary after the first rising stage.

500g strong white flour

I teaspoon sugar

I teaspoon instant yeast

I teaspoon fine salt

300ml hand-hot water

6 tablespoons olive oil

2 teaspoons coarse salt crystals

Equipment needed

baking tile (optional) or baking sheet

Makes I loaf

1 Place the flour, sugar, instant yeast and salt in a large mixing bowl and mix together. Pour in the hand-hot water and 3 tablespoons of the olive oil and gradually bring the mixture together to form a soft dough.

2 Transfer the dough onto a lightly floured surface and knead the dough for around 10 minutes until it feels smooth and supple. Cover the dough with a clean, damp tea towel and set aside in a warm place for 1 hour until the dough has risen and is roughly doubled in size. Break down the risen dough by kneading briefly. Place on an oiled baking sheet and press out the dough into a large oval about 1cm thick. Cover with a clean tea towel and set side for a further 30 minutes.

3 Preheat the oven to 240°C/475°F/ Gas 9. Preheat the baking tile if you are using one, or the baking sheet. Use your fingertips to press down into the dough, dimpling its surface.

4 Pour over the remaining olive oil, spreading it evenly over the surface of the dough. Sprinkle over the coarse salt crystals. Place the focaccia on the preheated baking tile or baking sheet. Bake in the oven for 15–20 minutes until golden-brown. Remove from the oven and cool on a wire rack, serving either warm or at room temperature.

Making sweet pastry

This rich, sweet pastry, a staple of pâtissiers, is ideal for sweet tarts. It can be made in advance, wrapped well and frozen for up to a year, ready to use as required. Do note that pastry recipes are traditionally measured by the amount of flour contained in the pastry, so the actual weight of the pastry here is 350g.

225g plain white flour

pinch of salt

I teaspoon caster sugar

115g butter, diced

I egg yolk

3-4 tablespoons cold water

Makes 225g pastry (enough to line a 25cm flan tin)

1 If making by hand, sift the flour and salt into a mixing bowl. Mix in the caster sugar.

2 Add the diced butter to the bowl and, working quickly and using your fingertips, rub the butter into the flour until absorbed.

3 Make a well in the centre of the mixture and place the egg yolk in the well.

4 Add 3 tablespoons of the water and mix together quickly and thoroughly with a knife until the mixture forms into a soft, sticky dough. Add some or all of the remaining water if required.

5 If using a food processor, place the flour, salt and caster sugar in the food processor and blend briefly to mix. Add the diced butter and blend thoroughly. Add 2 tablespoons of cold water.

6 Add the egg yolk, mix lightly with a knife and blend until the mixture comes together to form a soft dough, adding another tablespoon of cold water if necessary.

7 Once you've made the dough, either by hand or in the food processor, transfer it to a lightly floured surface and knead gently until the pastry becomes smooth and pliable. Wrap in clingfilm and chill in the refrigerator for 30 minutes to rest the pastry before using it.

Using your produce

Wild mushroom and garlic pizza

Strong white flour is higher in gluten than plain flour, and this will give your home-made pizza dough a lovely elastic texture.

For the dough

300ml warm water

1½ teaspoons active dried yeast

pinch of sugar

450g strong white flour, plus extra for dusting

1 teaspoon salt

2 tablespoons olive oil

For the topping

100g butter

500g wild mushrooms, wiped clean, trimmed and thinly sliced

3 garlic cloves, peeled and finely chopped

sea salt and freshly ground black pepper

1 mozzarella ball, thinly sliced

4 sprigs of fresh thyme

Makes 4 x 25cm pizzas

1 To make the dough, pour the water into a measuring jug, add the yeast and sugar and leave for 5–10 minutes in a warm place until frothy. Sift the flour and salt into a large mixing bowl, then stir in the frothy yeast mixture and the olive oil.

2 Mix well together, then tip out the dough on to a floured work surface. Knead for about 5 minutes until the dough is silky and elastic. Dust with a little flour, put into a bowl, cover and leave in a warm place for about 1 hour until the dough has doubled in size. Knock back the risen dough with your knuckles and divide into four pieces. Roll out each with a rolling pin and, using your fingers, stretch to a 23–25cm round.

3 Preheat the oven to 200°C/400°F/Gas 6. Place a lightly oiled baking sheet in the oven to heat up. Melt the butter in a large frying pan, add the mushrooms and sauté gently for about 2–3 minutes until thoroughly coated in butter. Stir in the garlic and seasoning and remove from the heat.

4 Brush the pizza bases with garlic butter taken from the mushroom pan. Scatter with the mozzarella and top with the mushrooms and sprigs of thyme. Brush with the remaining butter from the pan and bake in the preheated oven for 10–15 minutes or until the cheese has melted. Scatter with coarse ground black pepper and serve.

Variations:

Potato and rosemary pizza

Replace the mushrooms with 3 large parboiled, thinly sliced potatoes and the thyme with 2 sprigs of finely chopped rosemary.

Asparagus, bacon and egg pizza

Replace the mushrooms with 500g asparagus spears. Replace the thyme with 3 rashers of thick back bacon, roughly chopped. Add 1 medium egg cracked over the asparagus and bacon about 2 minutes before the end of cooking.

Wild rocket and cured ham

Replace the mushrooms with 1 bunch of trimmed whole spring onions. Replace the thyme with 4 thin slices of raw ham and add 75g wild rocket leaves on top.

Traditional tomato and garlic bruschetta

This is bruschetta at its simplest and best. Use only the best and freshest ingredients for this recipe, and for authenticity, you should use only the finest Tuscan extra virgin olive oil. The ripe tomato is just crushed in your hand and smashed onto the fresh bread, then eaten immediately.

4 large, very ripe tomatoes
sea salt and freshly ground black pepper
4 thick slices of sourdough (see page 56)
2 garlic cloves, halved
extra-virgin olive oil, for drizzling

Serves 4

1 Roughly chop the tomatoes and season with salt and pepper.

2 To make the bruschetta, grill, toast or pan-grill the bread on both sides until lightly charred or toasted. Rub the top side of each slice with the cut garlic, then drizzle with olive oil.

3 Spoon the tomatoes over the bruschetta and drizzle with more olive oil. Eat immediately with your fingers!

Chicken in a loaf

The idea for this recipe comes from southern Italy, where it is served cut in thick slices.

5 tablespoons virgin olive oil
1.35kg chicken, cut into pieces
500ml chicken stock
1 loaf of granary bread (see page 52), baked as a round
30g shelled almonds, toasted
30g shelled pistachios
2 eggs
juice of 1 lemon
45g capers, drained
bunch of flat-leaf parsley, chopped
salt and freshly ground black pepper

Equipment needed
food processor

Serves 6–8

1 Using a heavy-based pan that has a tight-fitting lid, heat 3 tablespoons of the oil over a medium heat and brown the chicken pieces all over. Pour in 250ml of the stock and cook until the chicken is tender, adding more stock if the pan looks in danger of drying out. Drain the chicken and leave it to cool, reserving the stock.

2 Preheat the oven to 180°C/350°F/Gas 4. Prepare the bread 'dish' and 'lid' by cutting the loaf in two horizontally, about one-third down from the top. Hollow it out carefully so as not to tear the crust, keeping the soft dough from the centre. Brush the crust all over, both inside and out, with the remaining olive oil.

3 Put both the almonds and pistachios in a food processor along with the dough from inside the loaf and whiz until reduced to the texture of fine crumbs. With the machine still running, slowly add the rest of the stock, the eggs and lemon juice. The mixture should be quite runny, so add an extra tablespoon of stock if necessary.

4 When the chicken is cool enough to handle, skin it and remove the flesh from the bones. Cut the meat into small pieces and stir in the capers and parsley, followed by the sauce. Season and spoon the mixture into the prepared bread crust. Cover with the lid and bake in the oven for 20 minutes or until golden. Serve hot or cold.

Leaf salad with vinaigrette and croûtons

Croûtons add a deliciously crispy contrast in texture to a salad and can be made from any bread, including leftover, stale slices. These croûtons would also be delicious in a soup.

2 little gem lettuces, washed and torn
1 butterhead lettuce, washed and torn
½ frisée lettuce, washed and torn
good handful of purslane, washed and torn
pinch of sea salt

For the croûtons
2 thick slices of granary bread, crusts removed (see page 52)
1 garlic clove, peeled
1 tablespoon olive oil
15g butter

For the creamy vinaigrette
1 tablespoon single cream
2 teaspoons sherry vinegar
5 tablespoons olive oil
freshly ground black pepper

Serves 4

1 Place all the leaves in a large salad bowl, mix together and scatter with the salt.

2 Meanwhile, to make the croûtons, cut the slices of bread into small cubes. Rub the inside of a frying pan with the garlic clove, heat the olive oil together with the butter in the pan and fry the bread cubes for 4–5 minutes, turning them over until evenly crisp and golden. Drain on kitchen paper.

3 To make the dressing, combine the cream with the sherry vinegar and beat in the olive oil. Pour over the salad leaves, toss together well and finish off with freshly ground pepper. Scatter the croûtons on top of the dressed salad.

Apple betty with dried cranberries

A traditional American recipe with very humble origins, it is always made with apples, but not necessarily dried cranberries. Just like English bread pudding, it is an economic way to use up stale bread, but it tastes even better if you use fresh white bread or even brioche.

900g tart eating apples, such as Cox's or Granny Smith, peeled, cored and diced

1 teaspoon ground cinnamon

1 tablespoon finely grated orange zest

75ml fresh apple or orange juice

100g dried cranberries

375g breadcrumbs (see page 52)

85g unsalted butter, melted

80g shelled pecans, chopped

75g light soft brown sugar

2 tablespoons unsalted butter, cut into pieces

whipped cream, to serve

Serves 4–6

1 Preheat the oven to 190°C/375°F/Gas 5.

2 Combine the apples, cinnamon, orange zest, apple juice and cranberries in a large bowl. Toss gently with your hands to mix and set aside.

3 In a separate bowl, combine the breadcrumbs and melted butter and mix well. Spread about one-third of the buttered breadcrumbs in the bottom of a well-buttered baking dish. Add the pecans and sugar to the remaining crumbs and mix to combine.

4 Put half of the apple mixture on top of the breadcrumbs in the baking dish. Top with half the breadcrumb and pecan mixture and top this with the remaining apple mixture. Finish with the remainder of the breadcrumb and pecan mixture. Dot with the butter and bake in the preheated oven for 30–40 minutes, until golden and crisp. Serve warm with whipped cream.

Apple tart

Apple tart is a classic use for sweet pastry, but this recipe represents a slight departure. The combination of apples and vanilla is divine, so I have added a layer of vanilla-scented apple purée. Serve warm or at room temperature with sweetened crème fraîche, whipped cream or vanilla ice cream.

225g sweet pastry, chilled and rested (see page 60)

3 mild eating apples, such as Golden Delicious, peeled, cored and sliced

1 tablespoon unsalted butter, melted

1 tablespoon sugar

sweetened crème fraîche, whipped cream or vanilla ice cream, to serve

For the apple and vanilla purée

3 apples (any variety), peeled, cored and diced

1 vanilla pod, split lengthways

2–4 tablespoons sugar (depends on tartness of apples)

2 teaspoons unsalted butter

Equipment needed

food processor

blender or food mill

27cm tart tin with a removable base

Serves 6–8

1 Preheat the oven to 190°C/375°F/Gas 5 and generously butter the tart tin.

2 Roll out the rested pastry into a circle about 6mm thick and slightly larger than the tin. Line the tin with it, trim the edges, prick the bottom with a fork and cover with greaseproof paper weighted down with some baking beans. Bake blind in the preheated oven for 15 minutes. Remove from the oven and leave to cool slightly.

3 To make the apple purée, put the diced apples, vanilla pod, sugar and butter in a saucepan with 3–4 tablespoons water.

Cook gently for about 10–15 minutes, stirring often until soft and adding more water if necessary. Use the tip of a small knife to scrape the seeds out of the vanilla pod, then discard the pod.

4 Transfer the mixture to a food processor, blender or food mill and purée until smooth.

5 Spread the purée evenly in the pastry case. Carefully arrange the apple slices in a neat circle around the edge; they should be slightly overlapping but not completely squashed together. Repeat to create an inner circle, trimming the slices slightly so that they fit, going in the opposite direction from the outer circle. Brush with melted butter and sprinkle over the sugar.

6 Bake in the oven until just browned and tender, 25–35 minutes. Serve warm or at room temperature with sweetened crème fraîche, whipped cream or vanilla ice cream.

Rhubarb and marmalade open tart

Rhubarb tends to collapse into a 'mush' when cooked and can spoil the pastry in a tart. To prevent this, dry-fry it first in sugar for just long enough to let its juices start to run but keeping it firm enough to stand the pieces upright in the tart.

15g unsalted butter, plus extra for greasing
225g sweet pastry, chilled and rested (see page 60)
450g rhubarb
2 tablespoons caster sugar
4 tablespoons coarse marmalade
1 tablespoon whisky

Equipment needed
20cm tart tin or 4 individual tart tins with removable bases

Serves 4–6

1 Preheat the oven to 190°C/375°F/Gas 5 and generously butter the tart tin or individual tart tins.

2 Roll out the rested pastry into a circle about 6mm thick and slightly larger than the tin. Line the tin(s) with it, trim the edges, prick the bottom(s) with a fork and cover with greaseproof paper weighted down with some baking beans. Bake blind in the preheated oven for 15 minutes. Remove from the oven and leave to cool slightly. Turn up the oven to 230°C/450°F/Gas 8.

3 Meanwhile, cut the rhubarb into 5cm lengths. Put them into a saucepan with the sugar and cook gently over a low heat for about 5–7 minutes, shaking the pan occasionally, until the rhubarb releases some of its juices but is still firm enough to handle. Strain, reserving the juices, and leave to cool.

4 When the pastry is slightly cooled, use a pastry brush to paint the base(s) and sides with 2 tablespoons of the marmalade. Stand the pieces of rhubarb upright in the tin(s), packing them in tightly, dot the top(s) with the butter, cover with greaseproof paper and bake in the preheated oven for about 15 minutes. Remove from the oven and leave to cool slightly.

5 To make the glaze: in a saucepan boil the rhubarb juices over a high heat to reduce to about 1 teaspoon. Stir in the remaining marmalade and the whisky and, stirring constantly, continue boiling to reduce by about half. Using a pastry brush, paint the glaze over the top of the fruit and allow to cool before serving.

Chapter 3

THE SWEETSHOP

For centuries, sweets were luxuries, made for and enjoyed by a wealthy elite. The craft of confectionery was considered a special skill characterised by creativity and inventiveness. Sweets may now be enjoyed by all, but those hand-made with the finest ingredients still stand out from the crowd.

Sugar and chocolate are at the heart of Western confectionery today, but the earliest known sweetener was honey, known to have been harvested from the hives of wild bees at least 10,000 years ago. Although honey is always sweet, its flavour depends on the blossom from which the bees have gathered nectar, as each flower has its own aromatic qualities. Honeys range enormously in taste and colour, from the mild sweetness of a clover honey to the dense, dark tang of chestnut honey.

Sugar, however, was to replace honey in its role as a prized sweetener. Sugar cane, a tall grass with a sweet-tasting juice, has a long history of cultivation in Asia. The first reference to solid sugar, made by boiling down the sugar cane juice until it crystallised, is on a Persian tablet of 510 BCE. The knowledge of, and taste for, sugar spread from the Middle East to Western Europe, where sugar was to be a luxury product until the eighteenth century. In contrast to its sweet,

pleasurable image, however, is the stark reality that the market for sugar fuelled the slave trade, with Africans transported in huge numbers to the Americas to work on sugar cane plantations. Other sources of sweetness include sweet saps, such as North America's maple syrup or Scandinavia's birch syrup. The nineteenth century saw the discovery that sugar could also be produced from a European vegetable – the sugar beet. Today, sugar from both beet and cane is cheap and widely available.

Nowadays, we take it for granted that chocolate is a key ingredient in confectionery, but for much of its history chocolate was consumed as a beverage, rather than in the solid form with which we are so familiar today. Chocolate is derived from the bitter-tasting beans of the cacao tree (*Theobroma cacao*), which is indigenous to Latin America. There are several varieties of cacao trees, with three main groups cultivated for use in the chocolate industry: Criollo,

Forastero and Trinitario. Criollo, low yielding and susceptible to disease, produces the rarest and most highly prized cacao beans, noted for their delicate flavour. In contrast, Forastero is a robust, high-yielding variety with a slightly bitter flavour, which provides the bulk of the world's cacao. A hybrid of Criollo and Forastero, Trinitario is more flavourful than Forastero and more resistant to disease than Criollo. Both the Mayan and Aztec civilisations valued cacao. The Spanish colonists who conquered Central America in the sixteenth century brought the cacao bean back to Europe, grinding the beans into a paste from which they made a drink called chocolate, which was prized as an expensive novelty.

Technological advances during the eighteenth and nineteenth centuries saw the rise of eating chocolate. A key stage in this process was the invention by a Dutchman, van Houten, of a screw press, patented in 1828, which separated cocoa butter (the fat found naturally in cacao beans) from the chocolate paste, leaving behind cocoa powder. Following this came the discovery that cocoa butter could be mixed with ground cacao beans to make a smooth paste that was solid when cool, but melted in the mouth – in short, the discovery of eating chocolate.

Understanding how to work with sugar and chocolate is the key to producing your own sweets and chocolates successfully at home. As with baking, the art of confectionery requires precision and an eye for the details of the process.

Above far left: Sugar cooked to the soft ball stage
Above centre left: Shavings of chocolate used for decoration
Above centre right: Raw cocoa beans
Above right: The finest chocolate has a cocoa content of at least 70%

Sugar

Sugar's remarkable range of properties makes it an extraordinarily versatile ingredient. When heated with water, sugar melts into a syrup. Heating this syrup to different temperatures produces confectionery with a range of textures, from soft, yielding fudge or toffees to hard lollipops or brittle praline.

There are many different types of sugars to choose from, with differences arising from the degree of refining and the size of sugar crystal. The extraction of sugar from the juice of sugar cane or beet results in a sticky black syrup called molasses. White sugar is made by removing the molasses entirely, while brown sugars, ranging in colour from golden to dark brown, retain varying amounts of molasses. The more molasses a sugar contains, the darker the colour, the stickier the crystals and the stronger the flavour, with, for example, dark brown soft sugar having a more pronounced taste than light brown soft sugar.

When it comes to making confectionery, fully refined white sugars, which have no taste other than sweetness, are extremely versatile. White sugar rather than brown is the best to caramelise, as you can judge the different stages by the colour the sugar turns to as it moves from pale gold to dark brown. Brown sugars, with their more pronounced taste, are often used to give extra flavour to confectionery such as toffees and fudges. Sugar sweets also have additional flavourings, such as peppermint, coffee or citrus fruits.

Sugar syrup is the base of most sweets. This is made by mixing sugar and water and heating it to different temperatures (see page 86) to produce the required texture and flavour. The deliberate introduction of 'interfering agents', such as liquid glucose or lemon juice, to inhibit crystallisation is another way in which different textures are created. Working rapidly at the 'soft crack' stage (see page 86), sugar syrup is pulled and stretched to create opaque, open-textured humbugs, whilst 'hard crack' syrup is twisted into traditional barley sugar twists. Simply stirring the syrup at various stages is another way of affecting the resulting end texture.

Toffees

Toffees can be made in a number of ways, with the syrup cooked to the 'soft ball' stage for caramels and soft toffees or to the 'hard ball' stage for hard toffees. The syrup is often enriched with the addition of butter or cream, and may be flavoured with treacle or rum. Usually the toffee syrup is simply poured out into a tin or onto a slab and left to cool, marked into squares when just hardened, then broken into smaller pieces.

Fudge

In order to make fudge, sugar syrup is traditionally enriched by adding butter, cream or milk. This syrup is then cooked until it reaches the 'soft ball' stage (see page 86). How the fudge is treated at this stage will affect its texture. For a firm-textured, granular fudge, the mixture is beaten vigorously while still hot. Allowing the fudge mixture to cool and crystallise first before beating it results in fudge with a smoother texture.

Opposite and right: An assortment of vanilla, cherry and walnut and chocolate fudge

Marshmallows and nougat

Marshmallows are made by boiling sugar syrup until it reaches the 'hard ball' stage (see page 86). The syrup is then combined with other ingredients, such as gelatine, whisked egg whites or glucose syrup, and whisked until light – a process that incorporates air into the mixture and gives marshmallows their characteristic fluffy texture. Nougat is made similarly, though often with the addition of nuts, with the nougat mixture spread out in an even layer and weighted down to compress it, so producing a denser, chewier texture than that of marshmallows.

Lollipops

Hard sugar-based sweets, such as lollipops, are produced by taking syrup to the 'hard crack' stage (see page 86), with different flavourings and colourings added to the base syrup as required.

Praline and nut brittles

Caramelisation is achieved at the highest temperatures on the sugar stages chart (see page 86). As the sugar caramelises, it creates distinctive flavours, the sugar becoming darker in appearance and more bitter in flavour the longer it is caramelised. Praline and nut brittles are made in this way.

Crystallised flowers

To make crystallised flowers, traditionally rose petals and violets, brush the flowers or petals with an egg white or a solution of a natural resin called gum arabic, then sprinkle them with caster sugar and set them aside to dry in a warm place or an oven on a very low heat.

Above left: Marshmallows dusted with icing sugar and cornflour
Above right: Lollipops made with button-shaped moulds
Right: An assortment of candied fruits

Candied fruits and nuts

Sugar syrups are also key to candied fruits and nuts –
a historic way of both preserving fruits and nuts and
transforming them into luxurious treats that have been
enjoyed for centuries. This is a time-consuming process,
which takes place over days. The first stage sees firm-
textured fruits, such as citrus fruits, stone fruits such as
plums, apricots or slices of pineapple or chestnuts,
poached in the syrup, then immersed in a strong sugar
syrup and left for 24 hours. Each following day, the
fruit are removed from the syrup, which is then further
sweetened and boiled down before the fruit are
immersed in it again, until finally set aside to dry.
This gradual process allows the fruit or nut to become
saturated with the syrup while preserving a soft
texture. A final coating in caster sugar creates
crystallised fruit, while dipping in syrup creates
smooth-coated glacé fruit.

Chocolate

By the time chocolate reaches your kitchen, it has already undergone a complex process of transformation, from the raw cacao bean to the dark, smooth substance we know as chocolate. Unlike sugar, which had a long history of use before mechanisation, chocolate's comparatively recent usage in confectionery is closely linked to developments in manufacturing processes.

The process by which raw cacao beans are transformed into eating chocolate is a lengthy one. First, the beans are fermented, then dried, then roasted to develop colour and flavour, then ground into a liquid paste called cacao liquor or cacao mass. The cacao liquor can then be processed further to extract the cocoa butter and create cocoa powder. Plain chocolate is created by mixing cacao liquor, sugar and cocoa butter into a paste.

This mixture is then refined by being passed through rollers, then conched (stirred mechanically for a few hours to a few days to homogenise the chocolate and bring out the flavours), returning the chocolate to liquid form. The chocolate is then tempered by being passed through a very precise process of repeated heating and cooling, to stabilise the cocoa fat. Then it can be moulded into shapes such as bars.

The higher the cocoa content in chocolate, the less sugar it will contain and the more bitter the chocolate will taste – 100% chocolate is very bitter indeed as it contains no sugar whatsoever. Milk chocolate contains cacao liquor, cocoa butter, sugar and milk solids. Its lower cocoa butter content means it is usually softer in texture than dark chocolate.

Using good-quality chocolate with a high cocoa content of 60–70% is an excellent starting point for making chocolates at home. Experiment with different brands of chocolates and different cocoa content. Chocolate made by reputable producers will have a better flavour and texture than cheap chocolate because the latter is often made by substituting vegetable fats for costly cocoa butter.

Working with chocolate at home usually involves returning it to a liquid state by melting. Professional chocolatiers temper their chocolate before working with it. This slow process of heating and cooling produces glossy chocolate with a pleasing brittle snap and a good shelf life. The melted chocolate can then be poured into moulds and allowed to set, creating chocolate bars, hollow shapes or cases.

Left: Studies have shown that consuming small amounts of dark chocolate regularly can benefit the body's circulatory system

Meet the producer: Paul A. Young

Fizzing with energy and enthusiasm for his craft, Paul A. Young opts for a purist, labour-intensive approach to his chocolate making.

'Everything we do is handmade. For me, that's what being an artisan is about. Anyone can order pre-made fillings, pre-made shells and use a tempering machine. We temper on a marble slab; we don't have a tempering machine,' he explains. 'Tempering is the trickiest part to get right. You have to get it to the right degree, if not, you get bloomed chocolate, chocolate that's not shiny or cracked chocolate. I guess I'm very old-fashioned, but I don't trust thermometers. We know our chocolate is right by touch and feel, by sight. Each chocolate has its own character and texture. It takes a long time to gain this knowledge.' The advantage of this insistence on traditional crafts and the acquisition of skills is that Paul can achieve exactly the results he wants. 'The advantage of marble tempering is that I can balance the chocolate, adjust the flavouring.'

Fine ingredients are at the core of Paul's luxurious chocolate range. 'We buy the best chocolate we can, not cheap sugary stuff, and are as seasonal as possible when it comes to our flavours. Unrefined organic sugar – I don't like anything that's over-processed. I use the same French butter I've used all my pâtisserie career, which is very smooth and not over-heavy, and our eggs are always free-range. Our ganache only lasts seven days; we make it daily, working like a pâtisserie.'

Paul is known for his daring flavours, with his marmite truffle having a cult following. 'My flavours are very distinct; you know what you're eating. I always try to be true to the flavours. For example, our champagne truffle is just champagne and chocolate, no cream, no butter. I like a champagne that's not too dry and matched it with a very smooth chocolate. I don't want my chocolates to taste generic; you can get that processed, sugar-heavy taste. Everything should taste individual.' Inspired by the power of sweets and to be evocative, Paul's new direction is distinctly creative. 'My new signature chocolate is called burning embers,' he declares. 'It looks like a little bit of coal and I've flavoured it with chilli, cedar wood and pine, to make you think of sitting in front of a fire on a winter evening.'

Liquid chocolate is highly valued as a dipping medium, used as a coating for shelled nuts, candied fruits such as orange peel, raisins, marzipan, chocolate truffles, and flavoured fondant creams such as peppermint or orange. If making a casing, as an elegant finishing touch, the chocolate casing can be decorated in a number of ways, including using a confectioner's dipping fork to add textured patterns while the coating is still soft, finely piping on chocolate patterns or sprinkling on a decorative garnish, such as chopped cocoa nibs or chopped nuts. The use of edible stencils to add a coloured pattern to the flat, smooth surface of a square chocolate is widespread among professional chocolatiers.

Chocolate is the essential ingredient used in a ganache, classically made from a mixture of melted chocolate and scalded cream, sometimes with the addition of butter. Ganache is used to make truffles. The ratio of chocolate to cream affects the texture of the ganache, with a higher chocolate content producing a firmer ganache with a richer chocolate flavour. There are different ways of making the ganache filling – see page 82 for one classic method. The ganache can be flavoured in many different ways, classically by adding a small amount of alcohol, such as rum, brandy or champagne, direct to the ganache, or by infusing the cream with spices such as vanilla.

Meet the producer: William Curley

Known for his elegant and accomplished creations, chocolatier and pâtissier William Curley gained his expertise working as a pâtissier in Michelin-starred restaurants with top chefs including Pierre Koffman, Raymond Blanc and Marco Pierre White.

'Working with pastry, chocolate plays a large part in what you do, so you learn skills such as tempering,' he explains. 'When it came to setting up my own business, this background, where you don't compromise on the product or the ingredients, has really influenced me. I use the best ingredients in my chocolates and pastries: Amedei, which, in my opinion, is the finest couverture, good-quality cream, really good butter. There's a subtlety to my chocolates, and because we're using Amedei, we always want to be able to taste the chocolate, rather than overpower it with the flavourings.' There's also a characteristic intricacy to William's chocolates: Piedmont hazelnut contains a layer of crushed hazelnuts mixed with feuilletine crumbs, praline and chocolate, set, then topped with a gianduja ganache.

William works with his Japanese wife, Suzue, also an acclaimed pâtissier, and there is a distinctive Japanese element to the flavouring of their creations. 'It just came about quite naturally,' he explains. 'I started with the well-known, classic flavours, but began to push the boundaries a bit, using fresh herbs like mint, rosemary and lemon thyme. On a trip to Japan, I spent a lot of time looking at different ingredients there, brought some back and started experimenting with them: ingredients like Japanese black vinegar, sesame, yuzu. I wanted to be original, but not to shock for shock's sake. Probably our most surprising chocolate is my apricot and wasabi — a layer of apricot paste with wasabi ganache on top. You get the apricot first, fruity and slightly sharp, then the wasabi hit at the end, but not too much — you wouldn't want it to be too powerful.'

Sourcing the ingredients

Chocolate

As discussed, cocoa beans undergo an intricate and complex process to become chocolate. Even the most experienced chocolatiers work with chocolate that has already been refined. One guideline for judging the quality of the chocolate is to look at the cocoa content, with reputable brands declaring the level of cocoa content on the label. When choosing plain chocolate, many chocolatiers recommend looking for around 65–73% cocoa content. Bear in mind that milk chocolate, made by the addition of milk solids, will have a lower cocoa content than plain. Read the label to check that cocoa butter, rather than vegetable fat has been used – another indication of good quality.

Remember, different cocoa contents will produce varying results; a recipe that works with a high-cocoa content dark chocolate may not work as well if you substitute a low-cocoa content milk chocolate. Professional chocolatiers and pâtisseries use couverture chocolate, a chocolate with a high cocoa butter content, specially made for use as a coating chocolate. This will require tempering before use.

Sugar

'Unrefined' sugars retain a natural colour and flavour that more processed refined sugars lack. Look for the word 'unrefined' when choosing brown sugars, as inferior brown sugars are made by simply adding colouring to refined white sugar and lack the depth of flavour that true brown sugars have.

Match the sugar to what you are making. White sugar has a neutral sweetness that makes it a very versatile and widely used sugar in cooking. For a more distinctive flavour, look to unrefined sugars.

Types of sugar

Caster sugar A sugar with small crystals, around 0.1–0.3mm, which dissolve much more quickly than granulated sugar. Available as white and golden.

Demerara sugar A raw cane sugar, originally from Demerara in Guyana, this sparkling golden sugar has large crunchy crystals and is used to add texture as well as sweetness.

Granulated sugar A sugar that has medium-sized crystals, measuring 0.3–0.5mm. Available as white and golden.

Icing sugar This extremely fine sugar, with its powdered crystals measuring 0.01–0.1mm, requires only moisture rather than heat to dissolve it. It is classically used to make icing.

Jam sugar A sugar that contains pectin, a carbohydrate found in fruit that acts as a gelling agent helping jams to set.

Muscovado sugar Dark brown in colour, this fine-grained sugar has a sticky texture and rich, full flavour. It is the most unrefined of all sugars.

Preserving sugar Specially created for use in preserving, this sugar has large crystals (1–2mm in size), which dissolve very fast when heated, so cutting down on the risk of caramelisation and burning.

How to store

Sugar should be stored in a cool, dark, dry place. Moisture will affect its quality and texture.

Chocolate should be stored in a cool, dark, dry place, such as in an airtight container in a kitchen cupboard, where it will keep well. Dark chocolate has the best keeping qualities, while white chocolate (made from cocoa butter and sugar, but no cacao liquor) is the most perishable.

Left: Examples of William Curley's elegant chocolate creations

Techniques

Sugar and chocolate require very different handling and the few golden rules outlined below are a useful starting point for successful sweet-making.

Recommended equipment for making confectionery:
accurate scales
sugar or jam thermometer
bain-marie
cool surface for working on, such as a sheet of marble
long-handled confectioner's fork

Cooking with sugar

A sugar syrup (also called stock syrup) is the starting point for most sweets, from soft fondant centres such as peppermint creams to gaudy, glossy lollipops. To make your sugar syrup successfully, first dissolve the sugar thoroughly in the water, stirring it as it dissolves (see page 86). Once the syrup is boiling, however, DO NOT STIR IT until it reaches the desired temperature, as this causes crystallisation and interferes with the cooking process.

As the temperature of the sugar syrup rises, it reaches a range of stages that produce different results (see page 86). Investing in a sugar or jam thermometer to measure the temperature of your sugar syrup is a simple way to ensure that you know when you've reached the correct stage. Alternatively, you can test the temperature of the syrup by carefully checking how a small portion of the syrup behaves when cooled in water, a test called the 'cold water test' and a method used by confectioners for hundreds of years. The texture of the syrup, ranging from thread to caramels, tells you the stage the sugar has reached.

As the water content evaporates, the heating process accelerates, so you need to keep an eagle eye on proceedings at the later stages. Bear in mind that working with sugar syrups requires care, as as it can become EXTREMELY hot.

Cooking with chocolate

The key to melting chocolate successfully is that it should be a very gentle process because if chocolate gets too hot, it separates. It's worth remembering that milk chocolate has a lower separation temperature than dark, so requires especially low heating. The safest way to melt chocolate successfully is in a bain-marie, in a heatproof bowl suspended over a pan of gently boiling water or in a microwave. A simple but effective way to speed up the chocolate melting process is by chopping it into small pieces or grinding it in a food processor.

When working with melted chocolate, it is very important to avoid it coming into contact with water as this causes it to 'seize' and stiffen into a thick paste. Do remember when using chocolate as a coating that it will only stick to ingredients with a dry surface.

Right: A coating of dark chocolate being poured on a dome of chocolate truffle and a biscuit base

Making chocolate truffles

This simple ganache recipe is for hand-made truffles. The recipe adds a touch of alcohol, a traditional flavouring for truffles, but feel free to experiment with other flavourings such as coffee or vanilla extract, though bear in mind that you'd only need a few drops of a strong-tasting extract if you don't want to overpower the chocolate. Vary the coating ingredients, as listed in the recipe, for added visual variety.

8 tablespoons double cream

200g plain chocolate (70% cocoa solids), broken into small pieces

I teaspoon rum, brandy, Cointreau or Grand Marnier

2–3 tablespoons icing sugar, sifted, for coating

2–3 tablespoons cocoa powder, sifted, for coating

2–3 tablespoons finely chopped hazelnuts, for coating

Equipment needed

bain-marie

hand-held mixer

Makes 12–16

1 To scald the cream, place it in a small pan, bring to the boil, then remove from the heat and set aside until tepid. Meanwhile, place the chocolate in a bain-marie or a large heatproof bowl over a pan filled with simmering water and heat gently until melted, stirring now and then with a wooden spoon.

2 Once the chocolate has melted, remove the bowl from the heat. Gradually add in the tepid cream, stirring as you do so. Stir in the alcohol or other flavourings, mixing well.

3 Using a hand-held mixer, aerate the chocolate mixture by whisking it for a few minutes until it becomes lighter and stands up in soft peaks.

4 Take large teaspoonfuls of the truffle mixture and shape it into rough balls with your fingers.

5 Coat the truffles in the icing sugar, cocoa or chopped hazelnuts. Store in a lidded container in the refrigerator for up to 3 days. Remove an hour before eating to soften them slightly.

Making classic fudge

These creamy succulent squares always prove a popular delight. Serve plain or liven up the basic recipe with cherries, nuts, rum and raisin or vanilla (see below).

397g tin condensed milk

150ml milk

450g demerara sugar

115g butter

Equipment needed

shallow tin
(about 30 x 20cm)

sugar thermometer

Makes approx 750g

1 Put all the ingredients into a large non-stick saucepan. Heat gently, stirring with a wooden spoon, until all the sugar has dissolved. Bring to the boil and simmer gently for 10–15 minutes, stirring continuously until the temperature reaches 116°C (240°F) on a sugar thermometer or test using the 'soft ball' method (see page 86). Lightly grease the tin and line with baking parchment.

2 Remove the pan from the heat. Beat the mixture with a wooden spoon for 5–10 minutes, until it is thick and grainy and the shine is taken off. If adding other ingredients, stir them in now.

3 Pour the fudge mixture into the tin and use a sharp knife to score the surface into squares, taking care not to cut all the way through. When cool, cut into squares and remove from the tin. Fudge can be stored in an airtight container for up to a month.

For a different flavour, try adding the following ingredients at the beating stage:

Fruit & Nut: Add 40g each chopped glacé cherries and pecans.
Rum & Raisin: Stir in 115g chopped raisins soaked in 2 tablespoons dark rum.
Vanilla: Replace the demerara sugar with caster sugar and add 1 teaspoon vanilla extract or the seeds from 1 vanilla pod.

Making stock syrup

This simple sugar syrup, made with equal quantities of sugar and water, is the starting point for many different sweeties, from fluffy marshmallows to brittle lollipops. It can also be used for preserving fruit. The syrup can be flavoured with alcohol, which needs to be added once it has cooled.

Sugar Temperature Stages and Usage

Name	Temperature	Description	Usage
Thread	106–113°C (223–235°F)	The syrup drips from a spoon, forming thin threads in water.	Glacé and candied fruits
Soft ball	113–118°C (235–245°F)	The syrup easily forms a ball while in the cold water, but flattens once removed.	Fudge and fondant
Firm ball	118–121°C (245–250°F)	The syrup is formed into a stable ball, but loses its round shape once pressed.	Caramel candies
Hard ball	121–130°C (250–266°F)	The syrup holds its ball shape, but remains sticky.	Divinity and marshmallows
Soft crack	132–143°C (270–290°F)	The syrup will form firm but pliable threads.	Nougat and taffy
Hard crack	149–154°C (300–310°F)	The syrup will crack if you try to mould it.	Brittles and lollipops
Caramel	160–177°C (320–350°F)	The sugar syrup will turn golden.	Pralines

400g caster sugar

400ml water

Makes about ¹⁄₂ litre

1 Simply pour the water into a small saucepan, then add the sugar, so that the sugar can start to dissolve without burning. (Also see notes on page 80.)

2 Bring to the boil and simmer for 4–5 minutes, then remove from the heat and leave to cool. If you are adding alcohol or any flavours, wait until the syrup has cooled, otherwise it will just evaporate. The syrup can be stored in a sealed jar or bottle in the refrigerator for a month.

Making marshmallows

Home-made marshmallows bear no resemblance to mass-produced versions. Light, fluffy and soft as a pillow, they are made with the purest of ingredients. You can vary the flavour by adding freshly squeezed lemon juice or stir in fresh soft fruits, such as raspberries. Eat them on their own or dipped in a warm chocolate sauce.

vegetable oil

50g icing sugar, sifted

50g cornflour, sifted

9 sheets of leaf gelatine

200ml water

450g caster sugar

1 tablespoon liquid glucose

2 large egg whites

1 teaspoon vanilla extract

Equipment needed

shallow tin (about 30 x 20cm)

sugar thermometer

metal jug

electric whisk (optional)

Makes 30

1 Lightly grease the tray with a little vegetable oil and dust it with half of the icing sugar and cornflour. Soak the leaf gelatine in 140ml cold water.

2 Put the remaining water, caster sugar and liquid glucose into a heavy-based pan. Bring to the boil and continue cooking for about 12 to 15 minutes until the mixture reaches the 'hard ball' stage, which is about 127°C (261°F) on a sugar thermometer (see page 86). When the syrup is up to temperature, carefully add in the softened gelatine sheets and their soaking water. The syrup will bubble up, so take care not to burn yourself. Pour the syrup into a metal jug.

3 Whisk the egg whites until stiff, preferably with an electric whisk in a mixing bowl. Continue whisking while pouring in the hot syrup from the jug. The mixture will become shiny and start to thicken. Add the vanilla extract or any other flavours and continue whisking for about 5–10 minutes, until the mixture is stiff and thick enough to hold its shape on the whisk.

4 Pour the mixture into the prepared tin and smooth the surface with a wet palette knife if necessary to remove any peaks. Leave for at least an hour to set. If you want to cover the tray, use a food net, as clingfilm or foil will stick and you will lose some of your marshmallow.

5 Dust the work surface and the marshmallow with some of the remaining icing sugar and cornflour. Loosen the marshmallow around the sides of the tray with a palette knife, and then turn it out on to the dusted surface. Cut into squares and roll in the sugar and cornflour. Leave to dry a little on a wire rack. To serve, carefully place the marshmallows onto skewers and serve with warm chocolate sauce. The marshmallows can be stored in an airtight container in a cupboard for up to 2 weeks.

Using your produce

Candied orange peel

These are lovely to make and the aroma of the cooking oranges makes this a perfect winter activity. They also make great Christmas presents when tied together in bunches with pretty ribbon. The sugar syrup used here is a variation on the basic stock syrup used in many confectionery recipes (see page 87).

4 large oranges

275g caster sugar, plus extra for coating

1 litre water

300g plain chocolate (70% cocoa solids)

Makes about 60

1 Score the oranges into quarters using either a sharp knife or a citrus scorer. Peel the oranges carefully, trying to keep the peels intact. Set the orange flesh aside and use in a separate recipe. Using a sharp knife, cut away as much of the white pith from the peels as possible – don't worry if some remains. Slice the peel lengthways into strips approximately 1cm wide.

2 Put the sugar and water in a saucepan over a medium heat and boil for 5 minutes. Add the strips of peel and reduce the heat to a slow simmer on the lowest setting. Do not stir. Simmer gently for two hours until the syrup reduces to approximately one quarter of its original volume. Remove the saucepan from the heat and allow the mixture to cool. Once cooled, drain the peels.

3 Preheat the oven to a very low temperature, approximately 85°C/200°F/Gas ¼. Put some caster sugar in a bowl and dip the peels in the sugar, coating them evenly. Place them on a baking sheet lined with baking parchment and sprinkle with more sugar if necessary.

4 Place the peels in the cool oven for an hour to allow them to dry out. Check at 20-minute intervals to ensure that the peels aren't cooking. Alternatively, leave on a drying rack overnight. Once the peels are completely dry, scrape off any excess sugar clumps.

5 Put the chocolate in a bain-marie or a small bowl set over a saucepan of gently simmering water. Don't let the bowl touch the water. Heat gently until the chocolate has melted. Dip each piece of peel in turn into the chocolate at least halfway, then place the chocolate-coated peel strips on a wire rack and leave to set. Store in an airtight container.

Figs in vanilla syrup

These gorgeous fruits look magnificent in the jar, beautifully pink and jewel-like. Baking the jar in the oven will help the figs to keep. The syrup used here is another variation on the basic stock syrup (see page 87), only this time it is scented with vanilla and cinnamon.

50g sugar

$\frac{1}{2}$ vanilla pod

3cm cinnamon stick

220ml water

6–7 figs, halved

$\frac{1}{4}$ teaspoon citric acid

Fills a 500ml jar

1 Preheat the oven to 150°C/300°F/Gas 2. Place the sugar, vanilla pod and cinnamon stick in a pan and add the water. Stir over a low heat to dissolve the sugar, then bring to the boil and simmer for two minutes to make a syrup. Remove from the heat. Discard the cinnamon stick. Slice the vanilla pod in half lengthways, scrape out the seeds with a knife and add them to the syrup.

2 Pack the figs into a clean sterilized jar (see page 121) with the cut sides facing outwards. Push the vanilla pod halves among the figs. Pour the syrup over the figs to fill the jar, swivelling the jar to remove any air bubbles.

3 Wrap kitchen foil over the top of the jar and place it in the oven, on a baking tray lined with several layers of folded newspaper. Bake for 25–30 minutes, by which time the syrup will have turned a lovely shade of pink. Remove from the oven, discard the foil and seal tightly.

S'mores

This is one for the kids. S'mores are an American campfire classic, where graham crackers (American digestive biscuits), barbecued marshmallows and chocolate squares are sandwiched together to make a delicious, gooey taste sensation. You can use a sweet biscuit, such as langue de chat or almond thin, instead of digestives, although really any biscuit will do. You're bound to want 'some mores'.

16 biscuits, such as digestives or almond thins
8 pieces of plain chocolate
16 marshmallows (see page 89)

Equipment needed
8 metal skewers

Serves 4

1 Put half the biscuits on a plate and top each one with a square of chocolate.

2 Preheat the barbecue. Thread two marshmallows onto each skewer and cook over hot coals for about 2 minutes, turning constantly until the marshmallows are melted and blackened. Remove from the heat and leave to cool slightly.

3 Put the marshmallows onto the chocolate squares and sandwich together with the remaining biscuits. Gently ease out the skewers and serve the s'mores as soon as the chocolate melts.

Chocolate chilli-salted truffles

A spicy take on the traditional truffle, these salty chilli chocolate versions, rolled in Himalayan pink rock salt, are so divine you won't be able to stop eating them! The recipe is a variation on the classic chocolate truffle (see page 82), using butter instead of some of the cream.

220g plain chocolate (70% cocoa solids), roughly chopped
60ml single cream
15g unsalted butter
½ teaspoon confectioner's chilli oil (or more or less, depending on taste)

For the salted cocoa dusting powder
55g caster sugar
20g cocoa powder, sifted
1 teaspoon ground cinnamon
1 tablespoon Himalayan pink rock salt

Equipment needed
melon baller

Makes 40

1 Put the chocolate, cream and butter in a heatproof bowl.

2 Place the bowl over a pan of simmering water, making sure the water does not touch the bottom of the bowl. Once the chocolate has started to melt, stir gently until the mixture is smooth and creamy.

3 Stir in the chilli oil and pour the mixture into a shallow bowl. Refrigerate until firm.

4 To make the dusting powder, mix together the caster sugar, cocoa powder, cinnamon and Himalayan salt in a bowl.

5 When the chocolate mixture has set, scoop out small amounts with a melon baller and roll into balls. Toss the truffles in the dusting powder and serve.

White and black puddings

These may be puddings rather than sweets, but hiding in the middle of each of these indulgent delights is a creamier version of the chocolate truffle mixture (see page 82). Once baked, it turns into molten chocolate, making a dramatic contrast with the white chocolate sponge pudding that surrounds it. It is very important to use the best-quality white and dark chocolate you can find.

For the dark chocolate filling
75g plain chocolate (70% cocoa solids), chopped
80ml double cream

For the white chocolate sponge
100g white chocolate, chopped
175g unsalted butter, at room temperature
150g golden caster sugar
3 large eggs, beaten
250g self-raising flour, sifted
pinch of salt
½ teaspoon vanilla extract
about 4 tablespoons milk
single cream, to serve

Equipment needed
ice cube tray
6 small (7.5cm diameter) pudding moulds

Serves 6

1 Oil six holes of the ice cube tray. Put the plain chocolate in a heatproof bowl set over a pan of simmering water and melt gently (do not let the base of the bowl touch the water). Remove the bowl from the heat and stir until just smooth. Stir in the cream, then pour into the oiled holes in the ice cube tray to make six 'cubes'. Freeze for at least an hour.

2 Preheat the oven to 180ºC/350ºF/Gas 4. Grease the pudding moulds.

3 When you are ready to make the pudding, melt the white chocolate as above. When melted and smooth, leave to cool.

4 Put the butter in a bowl and beat until creamy, then gradually beat in the sugar. When the mixture is very light and fluffy, beat in the eggs, 1 tablespoon at a time, beating well after each addition. Using a large metal spoon, carefully fold in the flour and salt, then the melted chocolate, vanilla extract and just enough milk to give the mixture a firm dropping consistency. Spoon into the prepared moulds to fill by about half. Turn out the dark chocolate cubes, put one into the centre of each mould, then fill with more sponge mixture to three-quarters full.

5 Stand the moulds in a roasting tin, cover loosely with well-buttered foil and bake for 25 minutes, or until just firm to the touch. Run a round-bladed knife inside each mould to loosen the puddings, then carefully turn out onto individual plates. Serve with cream.

Note: The chocolate filling should be made at least 1 hour before making the sponge, and can be kept in the freezer for up to a week.

Chocolate maple fudge

This variation on the classic recipe (see page 84) is a rich and decadent fudge for those with the sweetest of teeth to serve as a pick-me-up with mid-morning coffee or after dinner with a chocolate liqueur. Nibble a chunk and let it melt on your tongue – heaven! If you don't have a sugar thermometer, boil the sugar mixture for 5–7 minutes to the 'soft ball' stage (see page 86).

500g golden granulated sugar

100ml maple syrup

150ml milk or double cream

150g unsalted butter, cubed

150g plain chocolate (60–70% cocoa solids), broken into pieces

2 teaspoons vanilla extract

salt crystals

Equipment needed

sugar thermometer (for best results)

shallow 18cm square (or similar-sized rectangular) tin

Makes about 800g

1 Have a large bowl of cold water ready in the sink. Grease the tin.

2 Put the sugar, maple syrup, milk, butter and chocolate in a large, heavy-based pan and stir over gentle heat, without boiling, until the sugar has dissolved.

3 Bring the mixture to the boil and boil hard until you reach 116°C (240°F) on a sugar thermometer, stirring every now and then to prevent it catching.

4 As soon as you reach this temperature, remove the pan from the heat and dip the base in the bowl of cold water to stop the mixture cooking. Add the vanilla extract and beat well with a wooden spoon until the fudge becomes thick and creamy, with a grainy texture. Pour into the tin, smooth the surface and leave to cool for five minutes. Press some salt crystals all over the fudge.

5 When it is almost set, score squares in the surface of the fudge with the tip of a sharp knife. When completely cold, turn out and cut into squares.

Variation: For a nutty alternative, fold in 100g chopped walnuts or pecans immediately after beating the fudge.

Jewel-coloured lollipops

These lollipops are great fun. They use another variation on the stock syrup (see page 87), this time using very little water so they harden up nicely. You don't have to make them with moulds: when the sugar cools slightly, it becomes easy to mould into any shape. A fantastic treat for children!

200g granulated sugar

85g liquid glucose

food colourings

food flavourings, such as lemon juice, orange blossom water, strawberry flavouring, peppermint flavouring or rose water

Equipment needed

lollipop moulds and sticks

sugar thermometer

Makes about 16 depending on the size of the mould

1 Wash, dry and butter the lollipop moulds, if using. If you don't have moulds, you can use a silicone sheet or buttered greaseproof paper.

2 Mix the sugar, liquid glucose and 4 tablespoons of water in a saucepan. Cook over a medium heat, stirring with a wooden spoon until the mixture comes to the boil. To prevent sugar crystallization, use a pastry brush dipped in cold water and brush down the sides of the pan at regular intervals.

3 Boil the mixture without stirring until it reaches 149°C (300°F) on a sugar thermometer. Remove from the heat. Mix in a few drops of food colouring and any flavouring: use 1 tablespoon of lemon juice for the yellow lollies, 1 tablespoon of orange blossom water for the orange lollies and 1 tablespoon of strawberry flavouring for the red lollies.

4 Put the lolly sticks into the moulds and then carefully pour the mixture into each mould, ensuring that it doesn't spill over the top. If you don't have moulds, use a teaspoon to gently spoon and shape a lolly on a silicone sheet or greaseproof paper. Set aside and leave to cool at room temperature.

5 If storing, wrap the lollipops individually in cellophane or greaseproof paper and place in an airtight container.

Rocky road sundae

This cheerful combination of nuts, chocolate, marshmallows and glacé cherries is the perfect pick-me-up for anyone with the blues. Said to have been designed originally to cheer people up in the American depression of the 1930s, this sundae is guaranteed to bring a smile to your guests' faces.

For the chocolate sauce
2 tablespoons golden syrup
100ml double cream
100g dark chocolate
30g unsalted butter

For the marshmallow ice cream
650ml vanilla ice cream
50g marshmallows (see page 89), chopped
100g glacé cherries, chopped
30g toasted coconut flakes

For the chocolate crunch ice cream
650ml chocolate ice cream
100g chocolate biscuits, crushed
55g salted peanuts

To finish
chocolate vermicelli, to sprinkle
halved glacé cherries, to decorate

Equipment needed
4 glass sundae dishes

Serves 4

1 For the chocolate sauce, place the syrup, cream, chocolate and butter together in a heavy-based saucepan and whisk over a gentle heat until the chocolate has melted and the sauce is smooth and glossy. Leave to cool.

2 To make the marshmallow ice cream, remove the vanilla ice cream from the freezer and leave it to soften slightly. Once the ice cream is pliable, stir in the marshmallows, cherries and coconut flakes. Place the ice cream back in the freezer if not using immediately.

3 To make the chocolate crunch ice cream, take the chocolate ice cream from the freezer and leave it to soften slightly. Once the ice cream is pliable, stir in the crushed chocolate biscuits and peanuts. Put ice cream back in the freezer if not using immediately.

4 To assemble, put scoops of the marshmallow ice cream in the sundae dishes. Drizzle over some of the chocolate sauce (warmed if liked) and add a scoop of chocolate crunch ice cream followed by a second scoop of marshmallow ice cream. Sprinkle with chocolate vermicelli and decorate with a few glacé cherries. Serve immediately.

Chapter 4

THE PANTRY

Preserving's traditional imperative has always been to make the most of seasonal plenty, while transforming the ingredients. A piece of farmhouse cheese with chutney, cold meats and pickles, bread with strawberry jam — many of our favourite food-pairings feature preserved foods.

Vinegar, oil, salt, sugar and spices all play a pivotal role in the making of preserves. Vinegar, which occurs naturally as wine sours, hence its name (derived from the French *vin aigre*, meaning 'sour wine'), has long been used as a preservative due to its acid content. Apicius, the famous Roman epicure, wrote of many different types of pickles using vinegar, which were much esteemed by wealthy Romans. Verjus, the acid liquid made from green grapes, was also used by the Romans as a pickling medium. There is also an ancient tradition of preserving pickled ingredients in oil.

Salt's remarkable preserving properties make it a valuable ingredient. Salting ingredients, by using either dry salt (known as dry-curing) or brine – a liquid salt solution – (known as brine-curing), before immersing them in vinegar, is a traditional stage in pickling. The salt is used to preserve the food, by drawing out its moisture as well as adding flavour. Brine is also a stand-alone preserving medium, with gherkins, for example, being first salted and then cured in brine.

When it came to making sweet preserves, honey rather than sugar was the original sweetener, with the Ancient Greeks and Romans preserving foods, such as quinces, in honey. As sugar was a costly ingredient for many centuries, preserves made with large amounts of sugar, such as jam, were a luxury until well into the nineteenth century.

Spices, noted for their keeping qualities, have long been used to also add flavour to preserves such as pickles, chutneys and jellies. Piquancy can be created by adding chillies, mustard seeds or peppercorns, for example, with fragrant herbs such as bay leaves, rosemary or tarragon each adding their own specific aroma and flavour. Spices are used either whole or ground, depending on the level of flavouring required, with whole spices adding a milder flavour. The advantage of adding whole spices, such as cloves, peppercorns and cinnamon sticks, rather than ground to preserves such as flavoured vinegars or jellies is that they will not cloud the liquid.

Nowadays, we have become used to buying preserves that would have been made at home just a couple of generations ago. There is, however, something rather appealing about making chilli sauce or strawberry jam in your own kitchen, using good-quality ingredients and experimenting with different flavours, rather than buying a mass-produced version from a supermarket.

Artisanal producers know the value of making jams or chutneys in small batches because this domestic scale of production allows you to keep a close eye on the process to ensure good results. Even today, in a time of plentiful food supplies and deep freezers, there is still a profound satisfaction to the process of transforming, say, a glut of fresh ripe tomatoes into a tomato sauce or turning windfall apples into chutney for enjoyment in the months ahead.

Above left: Rosemary-infused olive oil
Above right: Apricots in syrup spiced with vanilla and cinnamon
Opposite: Mozzarella and tomatoes preserved in oil

Preserving fruits and vegetables

Our rich heritage of preserving fruits and vegetables over the centuries has resulted in many techniques and recipes, from pickles, chutneys, jams, marmalades and jellies, to ketchups, cordials and fruit cheeses. Preserving offers the opportunity to create numerous diffferent flavours with the same basic ingredients.

Pickles

A traditional way of preserving food is by pickling it in a solution containing either a high acid or salt content, since both acid and salt discourage microbial growth and act as effective preserving mediums, with vinegar and salt as the two major ingredients. The simplest method of pickling vegetables in vinegar is to sprinkle them generously with salt or place in brine (a salt water liquid) to draw out their moisture, a process that helps the vegetables retain their

texture and also reduces the risk of bacterial development. The vegetables are then rinsed to wash off the salt, covered with either hot or cold vinegar and stored. In order for the vinegar to be an effective pickle, it should have at least 5% acetic acid content. The use of hot or cold vinegar depends on the texture desired, with the cold vinegar method producing a crunchier textured pickle. Extra flavour is created by adding spices, herbs and aromatics – such as peppercorns, cloves, bay leaves, tarragon, garlic and onion – to the vinegar.

Chutneys

Vinegar also plays a key role in the making of chutneys. The word 'chutney', which derives from the Indian word *chatni*, is used in the Western kitchen to mean a cooked preserve made from chopped vegetables or fruit or a mixture of both, cooked with sugar and vinegar. Long, slow cooking develops the flavour and allows the chutney to reduce down; a contrast of sour-sweet flavour and a thick texture are the two main characteristics of a 'proper' chutney. Remember, as it cools, the chutney's texture will further thicken so resist the temptation to overcook. Always allow several weeks for a chutney to mature and mellow.

Left: Pickled shallots in spiced vinegar
Right: A selection of jams, curds and marmalades

Meet the producer: Wendy Brandon

Having started making six sugar-free chutneys, made using concentrated apple juice, for a health food co-operative in Brighton 25 years ago, Wendy has expanded her range considerably to around 200 preserves, including jams, jellies, marmalades and chutneys. Despite offering so many products, Wendy and her team produce her preserves in the way you might at home.

'We make very small batches by hand,' explains Wendy. 'The reason for cooking jams and marmalades in small batches is that they cook faster. Quick cooking is important so that they keep their flavour and colour, and to make a fresh and vibrant-tasting preserve. I made up my mind from the beginning that even if I expanded, I wasn't going to change how I made my jam. I had no ambition to run a factory.'

Wendy carefully sources her ingredients, using 'old-fashioned flavourful' fruit varieties where possible and dried fruit as well as fresh due to their 'concentrated' flavour. 'Our marmalade isn't too sweet; I use a mix of sugar and concentrated apple juice and the apple juice gives a sharper edge. Making a jam is like making a three-legged stool; you've got to get the balance right between the sugar, the pectin and the acid content. It took a lot of trial and error to get my recipes right.'

On making jams at home, Wendy advises testing. 'The home cook often makes the mistake of looking at a pan of boiling jam that's liquid and cooking it for longer, but if you do that, you'll end up with a product that cracks teeth! You have to do a setting test. With time, you get a feel for the look of the jam, of how it bubbles and spits.'

Careful cooking is key to all her production. 'We simmer the chutneys for three to four hours, depending on the fruit. They must be properly cooked as you want all the elements — the fruit, vegetables, dried fruit, vinegar, sugar, spices and garlic — to come together as a whole. We fill our jars by hand, rather than using a filling machine as many people do, and this means we can keep our chutneys chunkier, with more texture. Some people also add starch to their chutneys to make them pass through the filling machine, but that dulls the flavour so it's something I would never do myself. So many mass-produced chutneys are so bland-tasting; people seem scared of flavour.'

Meet the producer: Seafares

Seafares, a company specialising in producing both cooked and raw-cured seafood, is the brainwave of former chef and restaurateur Nigel Bloxham. Nigel uses a method called sott'olio, traditionally used for both seafood and vegetables. The idea came from Nigel's experience in the fish business.

'I saw all this cuttlefish going out to Italy, then the Italians selling it back to us preserved in oil in jars and thought that someone should do that here,' says Nigel. 'We use an age-old way of preserving, which is particularly associated with the Mediterranean. Hundreds of years ago, when they wanted to keep wine good, people would simply pour a layer of olive oil over the top to seal it. Now, we didn't have a lot of oil in England, but we had butter, which we used in the same way, pouring it over food when the butter was liquid and letting it solidify and set to form a layer on top, so making potted meats and potted shrimps. It's all about keeping out the air. We use this method with rapeseed oil, which is a very healthy oil, mixed with a little olive oil for flavour.'

As well as the oil, vinegar is an important ingredient in the process. 'To help the food keep, you need a product with a pH content, that is an acid content, and for that we use white wine vinegar or cider vinegar,' explains Nigel. 'Using good-quality seafood is the starting point. We're in a great part of the world for sourcing really good, fresh seafood, with Brixham very close and the rest of Devon and Cornwall near by. We produce cold-cured seafood including sprats, sardines and mackerel using the escabeche or sousing method, where raw seafood is covered in wine vinegar so that the vinegar 'cooks' it. It is then covered with oil and sold as a chilled product. Our other products are hot-cooked in wine vinegar, then preserved in oil. You need to cook the seafood enough for the vinegar to penetrate, but not to overcook it, as otherwise it becomes tough. Depending on what we're making and which method we're using, the marinating stage can be just a few hours or a few days. When it comes to flavouring, we use very little salt and we sometimes add herbs or use herb vinegars. We're particularly known for our seafood salad, which is a mixture of cuttlefish, octopus, squid, prawns, mussels and clams with roasted red pepper.'

Ketchups

Today, one of the most familiar table condiments is tomato ketchup. The word 'ketchup' derives from the Chinese *ke-tsiap*, meaning a fermented fish sauce, and has come to mean a salty, liquid condiment with a long shelf life. Ketchups can be made from fruits, vegetables, nuts and tomatoes, obviously, and range in texture from thick to runny. As with chutneys, both sugar and vinegar are the key ingredients, with the addition of spices and aromatics such as onion, garlic or ginger to create flavour.

Sott'olio

There is an established tradition of preserving foods in oil, usually olive oil – a process the Italians call sott'olio, which means 'under oil'. Both seafood such as mussels and calimari and vegetables such as artichokes, peppers, mushrooms and aubergines are preserved in this way, with the process involving first cooking the seafood or vegetables, usually by boiling them in vinegar, then cooling them, before covering them with oil. It's very important that the oil does cover the ingredients to avoid decay. Ingredients preserved sott'olio have a subtle richness of flavour, and in Italy they are often served as an antipasto dish.

Flavoured vinegars and oils

Flavoured vinegar is made by steeping the flavouring ingredients in the vinegar for a period of time until it takes on the required flavour. Popular flavouring choices for vinegars include herbs such as tarragon, sage, thyme or mint and soft fruit, such as raspberries or blackberries. These flavoured vinegars are then used in salad dressings, with fruit vinegars also diluted with water to make a refreshing drink. Flavoured oils are made by adding spices, such as dried chillies, or dried herbs to a good-quality oil, such as an extra-virgin olive oil, and setting it aside to infuse for around four weeks. Depending on their flavouring, these flavoured oils are then used in dressings or as culinary oils.

Bottled fruits

Bottling fruit in a sugar syrup (see page 86) is a traditional way to store them. Another simple way to preserve fruit is to immerse them in alcohol with sugar – cherries in brandy is a classic example. This has the advantage of creating not only deliciously tipsy fruit, but also transforming the alcohol by infusing it with the flavour of the fruit. Generally speaking, firm-textured fruits such as cherries, pears or peaches, rather than soft berries such as strawberries, give the best results.

Above: A jar of carrot confit
Opposite: Nigel Bloxham uses only the freshest seafood caught daily in his sott'olio produce

Jam

Other than fruit and sugar, the third essential ingredient needed for jam is pectin, a carbohydrate that occurs naturally in fruits, which causes the jam to set. Certain fruits, including apples, quinces and various citrus fruits, are rich in pectin, whereas others, such as strawberries and raspberries, have a low pectin content. The level of pectin will also vary according to the ripeness of the fruit – it is at its highest just as the fruit ripens. High-pectin fruits are also added to low-pectin fruits, either whole or in juice form, to make a jam set. Lemon and orange juice and pips are often used in this way.

The process of making jam consists of first gently cooking the fruit in order to soften it, then adding sugar, cooking it until it has thoroughly dissolved, then boiling the mixture until the jam reaches setting point (see page 107). Sweeteners such as concentrated apple juice or apricot purée can be substituted

for sugar. The classic ratio of fruit to sugar is one to one, but this can be tweaked to taste, with many artisanal jam makers preferring a higher ratio of fruit for a deeper flavour. Some recipes suggest warming the sugar before adding it to the fruit to help it dissolve more quickly; this is easily done by placing the sugar in a cool oven (140°C/ 275°F/ Gas Mark 1) for a few minutes before adding it to the fruit.

The skill in making jam rests in a successful boiling stage – this is where timing is vital. If the jam is not boiled for long enough, it will be too runny, whereas if it is boiled for too long, it will darken and caramelise. There are a number of ways of testing when jam has reached its setting point. The plate test involves spooning a small amount onto a chilled plate. If the jam sets and forms a skin that wrinkles when pushed, then it is ready. Alternatively, test it using a

Meet the producer: England Preserves

Noted for its artisanal jams and chutneys, England Preserves was set up in 2000 by partners Kai Knutsen and Sky Cracknell.

'We grew up in homes where people made jams and we took what we did for ourselves and turned it into a business,' explains Kai. 'Essentially what we do is use a very high percentage of fruit. Most industrial jams are boiled for a long time, whereas we simply heat our jams to 90°C (194°F) to sterilise them and to increase their keeping properties. What we're trying to do is to keep the character and colour of the fruit. The flavour of fruit is incredibly delicate and if you boil the jam, you destroy that flavour. It's more of a modern style of jam making, rather than the traditional way of boiling things to death.' They take the same approach to their chutneys, cooking them for less time than is traditional.

'We harvest and blast-freeze our fruit, then make the jams in small batches using a steam-jacket kettle, which allows us to monitor the heat very precisely. Each batch will vary a little and requires attention

when cooking. We make a gooseberry and elderflower jam and you have to be careful not to let the elderflower overpower the gooseberry and also not to overcook it, so as to keep that very special gooseberry flavour. As an artisan food-maker, you're nurturing something from nature, not stamping industrial parameters on it. The jams we sell are no more than a month old and we like people to eat them when they're fresh, but the chutneys need a few months for the vinegar to mellow.'

As their company name suggests, they work with English fruit, other than French apricots and Spanish Seville oranges for their marmalade. So committed are they to sourcing locally that they are now growing their own quince trees from which to make their rich-tasting quince cheese. 'We met a lot of farmers through working on farmers' markets, so we have a network of growers that we use. Our damson jam is made with a mixture of damson varieties from Brogdale Farm and other Kent growers. It's my favourite of our jams. It has the sweetness of jam and the fruity sharpness of damsons; a beautiful taste of England.'

pre-warmed sugar thermometer – 105°C (221°F) is the temperature at which the jam will set.

Above left: The sharpness of gooseberry jam makes it a great savoury accompaniment
Above right: Pear jam with vanilla seeds dotted throughout
Right: Mixed fruit, or tutti frutti, jam

Jellies

Another fruit preserve requiring the presence of pectin is jelly, usually made with fruits naturally high in pectin, such as redcurrants or apples. The process of making a jelly from fruit is a slow one, since first the juice has to be extracted. To do this, the fruit is cooked with a little water until it has softened and releases its juices. The cooked fruit is then placed in a very fine muslin bag (a jelly bag), suspended over a container and left overnight, so that the juices drip out. At this stage do not be tempted to speed up this dripping process by squeezing the bag, as this results in cloudy jelly rather than the desired clear, sparkling jelly. The resulting juice is measured and sugar added to it at the usual ratio of 450g sugar to 600ml fruit juice. The mixture is gently heated until the sugar has dissolved, then, as with jam, brought to the boil and boiled until it reaches setting point (see page 107).

Fruit butters and cheeses

Whole fruits are the starting point for making the sweetened fruit purées known as fruit butters or fruit cheeses. A fruit butter is a fruit purée with a spreadable texture, while a 'fruit cheese' is a thick fruit purée with a solid, sliceable texture – Spanish membrillo, made from quinces, is a good example.

The fruit pulp left from making a fruit jelly (see above) can be used, as can fruit that is too ripe for a jam or jelly. First, the fruit is cooked until soft, sieved if needed to remove any skin or seeds, then finally cooked with sugar until reduced and thickened. The ratio of sugar to fruit for a fruit butter is 225g sugar to 450g fruit pulp, while for a fruit cheese it is 450g sugar to 450g fruit pulp. Classic fruits include plums, damsons, quinces and apples; all, incidentally, fruits naturally high in pectin.

Fruit cordials

Fruit can also be used to make traditional fruit cordials that can then be diluted to taste. For a cordial, the fruit needs first to be cooked gently in a little water in order to soften and release its juices. The fruit mixture is placed in a jelly bag and left to drip overnight. This juice is then sweetened to taste with sugar and heated gently until the sugar has dissolved, creating a fruit syrup.

Left: A rose-tinged jelly made from crab apples
Right: Blackcurrants are one of the most popular fruits to use when making cordials

Sourcing the ingredients

When choosing fruits or vegetables for home preserving, bear in mind that you should choose them at the appropriate stage of ripeness. When preserving fruits in alcohol, use barely ripe fruits because the process will soften them. The best pickles are made with good-quality produce that is ripe, but never over-ripe. Similarly, fruit for jams should be just ripe, as otherwise it is tricky to get the jam to set. Ripe fruits that are too soft for jam making give the best results for jellies and fruit cheeses, where extracting the juice is the starting point.

When it comes to choosing fruits and vegetables for home preserving, using good-quality produce is important, so pick through the fruits and vegetables that you want to use, discarding any that are damaged or decayed. Using ingredients when they are at their best, most abundant, cheapest and in season is the traditional imperative for preserving. Using up fruits and vegetables from your own or a neighbour's garden is a good starting point. Markets are a great source of competitively priced fresh produce, with farmers' markets and farm shops offering a chance to find traditional varieties of fruits and vegetables, grown for flavour rather than appearance. Many traditional ingredients for preserves grow wild and can be foraged for free, such as blackberries, cloudberries, crab apples, lingonberries and rowan berries – all excellent in preserves.

For preserves that require vinegar, a good-quality vinegar is recommended, with at least 5% acetic acid content. White wine vinegar is far more delicate than malt vinegar, so bear this in mind when choosing which type to use. This also holds true when deciding which sugar to use (see page 79). Preserving sugar is recommended for jam making as its large crystals make it dissolve slowly and reduce the risk of burning. Jam sugar, known as gelling sugar in the United States, has added pectin and citric acid to help the jam to set.

Left: Shallots are the key ingredient for the classic pickled onion

Types of vinegars

Balsamic vinegar This famous Italian vinegar, made from grape juice, is available as cheap, mass-produced versions or costly, artisanal, traditional ones. With its dark colour, limpid texture and pronounced sweet flavour, it can be added to chutneys such as onion marmalade. It should never be used as a pickling agent.

Cider vinegar Made from cider, this vinegar has a distinct apple flavour and is often used for pickling fruits or vegetables.

Malt vinegar Made from a type of beer created from malted barley, this has a strong flavour and is generally used for strong pickles such as pickled onions or eggs.

Sherry vinegar Made from sherry, this traditional Spanish vinegar has a distinctive sweet, nutty flavour.

Wine vinegar Made from either white wine or red wine and coloured accordingly, their delicate flavour means that wine vinegars are widely used in preserving. Wine vinegars made using the traditional, time-consuming Orleans method, where wine is carefully converted into vinegar in wooden barrels, are particularly esteemed for their depth of flavour.

How to store

Scrupulous care must be taken when sealing preserves, and they should be stored in clean, heat-sterilised containers. Always follow the recipe instructions regarding bottling, storage and consumption carefully. Bear in mind that food stored in vinegar or alcohol needs to be completely covered by the liquid in order to be thoroughly preserved. Well-fitting waxed paper lids are often recommended for all preserves. Press the lids onto the surface of the preserve when it is either very hot or very cold in order to disperse air pockets and to avoid moisture condensing on the lid, which would create an atmosphere in which moulds can thrive. Liquid preserves, such as cordials, stored in bottles with corks will gradually evaporate through the cork, so a wax coating on corks is advised to make them airtight. When using preserving jars, check that any fittings such as rubber rings haven't decayed.

Label your preserves clearly with the date of making and the contents. The general rule for storing preserves is to keep them somewhere dark, dry and cool, such as a cupboard, well away from any heat source.

Above: Almost any fruit can be preserved in syrup. Here are crab apples, orange slices, figs and cherries

Making vinegar

Making your own vinegar at home is very simple indeed. Using a fruit juice, such as apple or grape, gives a deep fruity flavour.

The fruit juice you select should be free of additives or preservatives and unpasteurised. Fresh apple or grape juices are good choices, ideally squeezed from your own fruit. By using grapes or grape juice, you create wine vinegar. If you use apple juice, you'll end up with cider vinegar. If the fruit juice has less than 10% sugars, it will produce less than 5% alcohol and less than 4% acetic acid in the finished vinegar and will be prone to spoiling.

To ensure success, especially for your first time, start by adding organic unfiltered vinegar from a health-food shop or use a vinegar starter or 'mother', available on the internet. After you have done that once, just reserve a cup or so of your own home-made vinegar to add to the next batch. This is the source of bacteria for the fermentation process.

750ml 'mother' unfiltered vinegar

750ml fresh fruit juice

Equipment needed

large glass jar or container with a wide mouth (don't use metal or plastic as the acid can interact with these materials and ruin your vinegar)

piece of muslin

string

coffee filter paper

small bottles with airtight lids

Makes 1.25 litres

1 Find a large glass jar with a wide, open neck that will allow you access to the 'mother' when it forms. Mix together the vinegar and fruit juice. If the fruit juice is below 10% sugar content, add a couple of spoonfuls of sugar. Cover the opening with a double layer of muslin to keep out the fruit flies (but be sure, they will come to it where ever you put it).

3 Keep checking the vinegar until it is as strong as you like it, or it seems to be losing strength. This can be any time from 6–12 weeks. Reserve some for the next batch.

4 Strain it through some coffee filter paper to remove the 'mother'. Bottle the vinegar in small bottles with airtight lids to reduce the chance of any residue of the 'mother' starting to work again (the bacteria need both food and air). Leave it for at least six months in the back of a cupboard before using (you could use it right away, but by leaving it you will have a smoother taste).

Note: When all the alcohol has been used up by the bacteria, they will start to feed on the acetic acid, producing water and carbon dioxide. This is why the vinegar starts to weaken and becomes prone to spoilage. You can stop all the action by pasteurising the vinegar by bringing it to the boil up to 70ºC (158ºF) to kill the remaining bacteria of all kinds before bottling.

2 Put the mix into a warm, dark place. An airing cupboard is great, as long as you have the cylinder well insulated. The temperature should be 24–29ºC (75–85ºF) in the storage area.

Pickling vinegars

If you want to produce vinegar for pickling, you will need to be more controlled in your production and will need to add in another stage so you can guarantee the alcohol content. This process is necessary because alcohol production is an anaerobic action and vinegar production is aerobic, therefore the two processes need to be separated to keep control of the alcohol production.

When making pickles, the subtle flavours of fruit and cider vinegars can be overwhelmed so most recipes ask for malt vinegar to be used. Malt vinegar is not really a vinegar in the truest sense as it is made from ale (a basic beer without hops that contains malted barley or other grains) rather than wine (vin). The best way to start making malt vinegar is to buy a beer-making kit that uses malted barley as its base. Don't worry if the kit has hops in the recipe as it will not harm the final 'vinegar'. The only thing you need to remember is the alcohol content of the ale needs to be between 5% and 7% by volume. Apart from that just follow the instructions supplied with the kit to make the ale and make the vinegar following the method on page 112, using the ale as the vinegar stock. Don't throw yourself in at the deep end by trying to make beer from grain and hops; you need to walk before you run.

For fruit vinegars, make a wine first from the fruit, so you can control the alcohol content, and then make the vinegar. Once again the easiest way to do this is to purchase a wine kit to make the first batch of wine, after that you can use the equipment to make wine from your own garden fruit. You can also purchase a traditional French-style vinaigrier online that will be great for making various types of fruit vinegar.

Things to remember are that the specific gravity of the juice at the start of the process should between 10 and 18 on the Brix scale and 0 when finished (0 = no sugar left in the vinegar stock). A good kit will contain a Brix hydrometer, which is very easy to use, but you need to follow the instructions closely. You will need to add some sugar to the fruit juice if the Brix reading is below 10.

Opposite: Bottles of home-made cider, red wine and white wine vinegar
Right: Experiment with different herbs and note the impact they have on the finished flavour

Flavoured vinegars

If you want to flavour your homemade vinegar, you can do this by adding your chosen flavour and leaving it to infuse for about six weeks. Never leave items in the vinegar for longer than six weeks as they can cause the whole thing to spoil.

Some things to try in vinegar are:
- raspberries
- blueberriess
- onion
- garlic
- basil
- strawberrie
- chillies
- dill
- oregano

Using your vinegar

While home-made vinegar can be good for dressing salads and general-purpose usage, its acidity may not be adequate for safe use in pickling and canning. Unless you are certain the acidity is at least 5%, don't pickle or can with it.

Making green tomato, raisin and mint chutney

This is particularly special chutney, as it has a sharp, clean flavour that is neither too cloying nor too sweet. This recipe is also a useful way of using up unripe or green tomatoes, which are too hard and bitter to be eaten raw and fail to ripen, even if left on a sunny window sill or wrapped in brown paper bags. As with all chutneys, make sure the ingredients are of a good quality and free of any bruises or blemishes.

1.5 kg green tomatoes, cut into dice

450g onions, finely chopped

450g raisins

450g demerara sugar

250ml cider vinegar (see page 112)

100g fresh root ginger, peeled and finely sliced

1 teaspoon cayenne

½ teaspoon salt

50g coarsely chopped fresh mint leaves

Equipment needed

large saucepan or preserving pan

4 warm, dry sterilised 575ml glass jars (see page 121)

waxed paper discs

Makes 4 x 575ml jars

1 Put all the ingredients except the mint in a large saucepan or preserving pan and bring to a simmer over a medium to low heat. Then leave to simmer uncovered for about 1 hour, stirring occasionally with a wooden spoon, taking care not to crush or break up the vegetables or to let the mixture bubble too fiercely.

2 Stir in the mint and simmer for a further 15 minutes, or until the vegetables are just tender but not too soft.

3 Have ready the sterilised glass jars and pack the chutney loosely into them. Cover with waxed paper discs and leave to cool overnight. The following morning, seal and label the jars and store them in a cool, dark place to mature for about a month before you even think of trying the chutney. Once opened, the chutney will last for at least 3 months if kept in the refrigerator.

Making sott'olio

A classic Mediterranean way of preserving food combines first cooking the ingredients in vinegar, then immersing them in olive oil. The results both look and taste fantastic.

Sott'olio requires particular care in preparation because while oil has preserving properties, it is not a preservative. It prevents spoilage merely by isolating the vegetables from the air, which means that the vegetables must be fully cooked (often in vinegar, as the acidity acts as a disinfectant) and transferred immediately into a sterile jar. This must be filled at once, then tapped briskly to dislodge any air bubbles. Never pack raw vegetables in oil as they can harbour bacteria on their surfaces, even if they have been well washed, which can flourish in the anaerobic (i.e. airless) environment of a sott'olio jar. Garlic in particular has been known to harbour the bacteria that cause botulism. When you open a jar of sott'olio, take care: if the lid is domed up, and there's a whisper of air escaping, discard it because it might not be safe.

2 medium aubergines

500g courgettes

500ml water

salt

375ml white wine vinegar
(see page 112)

5-6 small garlic cloves, sliced

6 anchovy fillets, chopped (optional)

1 teaspoon dried chilli flakes

1 teaspoon dried oregano

6 fresh mint leaves, roughly chopped

extra-virgin olive oil, for covering

Equipment needed

large strainer

some sort of heavy weight

2 warm, dry sterilised 450g glass jars
(see page 121)

Makes 900g

1 Start by removing some of the aubergine skin with a vegetable peeler, creating stripes. I personally like leaving some of the skin on for the chewy texture and great purple colour, but it's up to you. Cut the aubergines into 5mm slices widthways (they tend to hold their shape better the thicker they're cut). Salt each aubergine thoroughly and layer in a large strainer with a heavy weight on top (anything heavy will work). The idea is to press out all of the bitter juices from the aubergines, leaving you with just sweet flesh. Allow to drain for two hours until there is a pool of dark brown liquid below the strainer, then rinse and pat dry. Cut the courgettes lengthways into 5–10mm slices.

2 In a medium-sized saucepan, bring the water with some salt and 250ml of the white wine vinegar to the boil. Add the sliced courgette and cook for 4–5 minutes until tender, but still with a bite. Remove from the cooking liquor, reserving the liquor so you can repeat with the aubergine slices. They also take 4–5 minutes to cook and the aubergine will become bright and transparent when ready. It is better to do the aubergine last as the vibrant purple colour taints the cooking liquor.

3 Once both the courgette and the aubergine are cooked and drained, you can just pat them dry with kitchen paper. Add the vegetables to the sterilised jars. You can do a jar of each or mix them in layers.

4 All that is left to do is to make the dressing. Mix the garlic, anchovies, chilli flakes, dried oregano, mint leaves and remaining white wine vinegar with about 250ml olive oil. Once it is mixed, pour it over the vegetable in the jars. If they are not completely covered, just top up the jars with more olive oil. Tightly seal the jars, and they are ready to eat. They may be kept like this, refrigerated, for up to four weeks as long as the olive oil level is kept so that the vegetables are covered. Keep in the bottom of the fridge so the oil does not set, or just remove it from the fridge before you want to eat it so that it warms up and the oil becomes liquid again.

Making strawberry and vanilla jam

Strawberry jam is a real classic. This fragile fruit isn't a great keeper, so for the best jam, capture the fruit at its freshest, preserving it in recognisable chunks. Here the strawberries have been teamed with vanilla, the perfect partner to make a truly delicious jam. This recipe uses slightly less sugar than a traditional strawberry jam might and consequently has a softer set, which means if you are feeling really gluttonous, you can eat it straight from the jar. Swirl a few spoonfuls through a mixture of mascarpone and plain yoghurt for a fast pudding or dollop it onto a freshly baked scone – eating it quickly before the jam oozes away over the sides.

1 vanilla pod

1kg strawberries, hulled
(larger fruits halved)

750g sugar

juice of 3 lemons

Equipment needed

sugar thermometer

preserving pan

3 warm, dry sterilised 450ml
glass jars (see page 121)

waxed paper discs

Makes 1.35kg

1 Split the vanilla pod lengthways into four pieces and place in a bowl with the strawberries, tucking the pod pieces in among the fruit. Cover with the sugar and leave for 12 hours or overnight.

2 Pour the fruit, vanilla pod and juice into a preserving pan and add the lemon juice. Cook over a low heat until the sugar has dissolved, stirring only now and then so that the fruit stays intact. Turn up the heat and boil rapidly to reach setting point. Use a sugar thermometer to test for this – it should read 105° C (220° F) when placed in the centre of the pan. Skim with a metal spoon if necessary to remove any scum, or stir in a small knob of butter to help it disperse.

3 Remove the vanilla pod pieces, scrape the seeds out of them and add these to the jam, disposing of the pods. Stir the seeds through the jam.

4 Pour the jam into the jars, cover with a waxed disc placed wax side down and seal. The jam can be stored for at least 12 months if kept unopened in a cool dark place.

Note: To sterilise jars or bottles, wash them in hot soapy water, then rinse in clean hot water before drying. Next, put them in an oven at 110° C (230° F) for 20 minutes and use immediately, while still warm.

Making ginger and lemon cordial

This cordial, though not intentionally medicinal, is soothing and warming and is ideal to drink as a hot beverage if you feel a cold coming on.

2 lemons
50g fresh root ginger, bruised
1.2 litre water
sugar (for quantity, see step 2)

Equipment needed
clip-top or corked bottles or freezer containers

Makes about 750ml

1 Juice and thinly pare the rind of the lemons. Put the ginger and lemon rind in a pan with the water. Simmer gently for 40 minutes.

2 Discard the rind and ginger with a spoon before straining through a sieve into a measuring jug to remove any extra sediment. Add 400g sugar to every 600ml liquid and the lemon juice and stir over a low heat until all the sugar has dissolved. Bring just to the boil, then remove quickly from the heat.

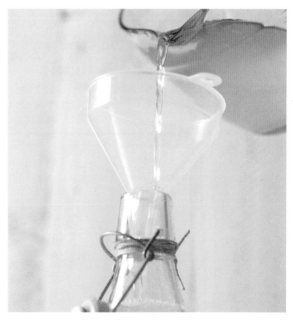

3 Pour the cordial into clean clip-top or corked bottles and sterilise. To do so, place a folded cloth or trivet in a large pan and place the bottles on top. Pour in cold water to cover the bottles up to the neck, then bring to the boil and simmer for 20 minutes. Once cooled, the cordial will be ready to drink. The cordial will keep for several months if stored in a refrigerator. Alternatively, pour the cordial into freezer containers, seal and freeze. This will sterilise the cordial and keep it fresh for longer.

Using your produce

Quick vinegars

If you are short of time, these two recipes will work perfectly well when making pickles and chutneys.

Pickling vinegar

1 litre cider or wine vinegar (see page 112) or malt vinegar

20g fresh root ginger, peeled and finely sliced

1 tablespoon each black peppercorns, mustard seeds, celery seeds

8 dried red chillies

2 teaspoons each whole allspice, whole cloves, coriander seeds

Makes 1 litre

1 Place all the ingredients in a bowl and place over a pan of simmering water, or use a double boiler. Allow the vinegar to warm through without boiling, then remove it from the heat and leave the spices to steep in the warm vinegar for 2–3 hours.

2 Strain the spices from the vinegar before using.

Sweet pickling vinegar

600ml white wine vinegar (see page 112)

200g sugar

1cm square piece fresh root ginger

1 tablespoon each whole allspice, black peppercorns

Makes 600ml

1 Place the ingredients in a pan and stir over a low heat to dissolve the sugar.

2 Turn up the heat and boil for 1 minute, then remove from the heat. Strain the spices from the vinegar before using.

Onion marmalade

Serve an onion marmalade with pâté, cold meats or sausages. If you like a contrast of textures, try mixing it with a mixture of onions, shallots and even a few white pearl onions.

3 tablespoons extra-virgin olive oil

900g onions, sliced

5 shallots, sliced

85g light muscovado sugar

salt and freshly ground black pepper

3 tablespoons honey

300ml red wine

75ml cider vinegar, pasteurised (see page 112)

handful of raisins

Equipment needed
4 warm, dry sterilised glass jars (see page 121)

Makes 4 x 300ml jars

1 Heat the olive oil in a large frying pan, and stir in the onions, shallots and sugar. Season with salt and pepper. Cover the pan and cook over a gentle heat for 30 minutes, stirring occasionally with a wooden spoon.

2 Add the honey, wine, vinegar and raisins. Carry on cooking over a very low heat, still stirring from time to time, for about 20 minutes or until the onions make a thick syrup.

3 Remove from the heat immediately and pour into hot sterilised jars (see page 121). Seal in the usual way and leave to stand for at least 2–3 weeks before even trying it. Once you have opened the jar, keep it cool in the refrigerator and it will last for at least 2 months.

Beetroot chutney

Beetroots are another vegetable that at the height of the season you either have none of or far too many, so chutney making (see also page 116) suits them well.

900g raw beetroot, peeled and coarsely grated
450g onions, peeled and chopped
700g cooking apples, peeled, cored and chopped
450g seedless raisins
1.1 litres pickling vinegar (see page 124)
900g sugar
2 teaspoons ground ginger

Equipment needed
stainless steel preserving pan
warm, dry sterilised glass jars (see page 121)

Makes about 2.75kg

1 Place everything in a stainless steel preserving pan and stir over a gentle heat to dissolve the sugar. Bring to the boil, then simmer gently for about 1 hour until the beetroot and onions are soft and the chutney is thick but still juicy, stirring occasionally.

2 Pour the chutney into the jars and seal. Once opened, keep in the refrigerator and it should keep for several months.

Piccalilli

The Edwardians were very fond of their chutneys and pickles, which were always taken with a cold collation of beef, tongue or ham.

450g green tomatoes, sliced

450g green beans, sliced

450g carrots, sliced

1 cauliflower, cut into florets

450g pickling onions, peeled

225g salt

3.6 litres water

50ml mustard powder

50ml ground ginger

20ml ground turmeric

1 teaspoon celery seeds

115g sugar

1.1 litres white wine vinegar, pasteurised (see page 112)

30g cornflour

Equipment needed

warm, dry sterilised glass jars (see page 121)

Makes 2kg

1 Put the vegetables into a large bowl and add the salt and water. Stir thoroughly and weight the vegetables so they are immersed in the water.

2 Heat the spices, sugar and 1 litre of the vinegar in a saucepan, and simmer, stirring occasionally, for about 5 minutes.

3 Rinse the vegetables and add them to the pan. Bring to the boil and simmer for about 15 minutes or until they are soft but still a little crunchy. Strain the vegetables, reserving the cooking liquid, and pack them quite tightly into warm sterilised jars.

4 Stir the cornflour into the remaining vinegar and add it to the cooking liquid. Bring to the boil and cook for a few minutes, stirring constantly until it has thickened.

5 Pour over the vegetables in the jars, leave to cool and then seal. Keep it in a cool for at least 6 weeks before eating to allow the flavours to mellow.

Pickled shallots

Pickled onions are a classic pickle and one that seems to be popular with children and adults alike. They go with just about anything, but a simple ploughman's lunch made up of a piece of crusty bread, a wedge of strong cheese and some pickled onions is a combination that is hard to beat. To be sure that your onions retain that initial crunch, they need to be marinated in brine for a few days before being packed into jars and covered in spiced vinegar. Apart from that, this pickle has to be the easiest there is and you should always keep a few jars on the pantry shelf.

1kg pickling shallots
250g salt
600ml pickling vinegar (see page 124)

Equipment needed
warm, dry sterilised glass jars (see page 121)
Makes 1kg

1 Place the shallots in a large bowl without skinning them. Make the brine by dissolving half of the salt in 1.1 litres water, then pour this over the shallots and leave in a cool dark place for 12 hours. Drain and skin the shallots.

2 Make up a second batch of brine using the remaining salt and the same amount of water, pour it over the shallots and leave for a further 2–3 days.

3 Drain and rinse the salt from the onions and pack them tightly into sterilised jars. Pour the pickling vinegar over them so that they are completely covered. Cover and seal the jars. The shallots will keep their flavour and crispness for up to six months after bottling.

Cherry jam

You can use a black cooking cherry, such as a Morello cherry, for this jam, or a paler dessert cherry, and the colour of your jam will vary accordingly. Note that, unlike the strawberry and vanilla jam (see page 120), here the fruit is cooked before the sugar is added. If you grow your own cherries (or strawberries, for that matter), make sure to pick them as soon as they ripen or else the birds will eat the lot before you get the chance. As with all jams, the jars should be sterilised before use.

700g cherries

500g sugar

1 tablespoon lemon juice

Equipment needed

cherry stoner

preserving pan

sterilised jars (see page 121)

Makes 900g

1 Pit the cherries using a cherry stoner over a basin to catch any juice. Place the stones in a piece of muslin and tie it into a bag with string. Put the fruit and juice into a pan with 2 tablespoons water and simmer gently until the fruit is just cooked.

2 Warm the sugar in a bowl in the oven on its lowest setting for around 20 minutes. Add the sugar and the lemon juice to the fruit and stir over a low heat until all the sugar has dissolved, then turn up the heat and boil rapidly to reach setting point. Remove the muslin bag and leave the jam for 5–10 minutes, then stir to redistribute the cherries. Skim if necessary.

3 Pour the jam into the jars and seal. It should keep for at least 6 months if kept, unopened, in a cool, dark place.

Plum and pear jam

Unlike the strawberries in the jam on page 120, ripe plums are full of natural sugar and pectin, so they can be used in one of the few jam recipes that needs absolutely no added sugar. You must, of course, use very soft ripe plums and pears in this recipe to achieve the right sweetness and set. It is therefore an ideal way of coping with a windfall, provided you cut out any bruises or damage from the fruit. This recipe is more like a purée than a true jam in texture, but it will keep for months, provided you store it in the refrigerator or in a very cool place.

900g ripe eating plums, stoned and halved

zest and juice of 1 orange

stick of cinnamon, crushed

2 cloves

250ml water

900g pears, peeled, cored and roughly chopped

zest and juice of 1 lemon

2 tablespoons honeyed sweet dessert wine (optional)

Equipment needed

preserving pan

sterilised jars (see page 121)

Makes 1.35–1.8kg

1 Put the plums in a preserving pan with the orange juice and zest, the cinnamon, cloves and water over a low heat and simmer for about 20 minutes, stirring frequently, or until the fruit is quite soft.

2 Add the pears along with the lemon zest and juice and sweet wine, if using. Simmer, stirring occasionally, for a further hour, or until the fruit has reduced to a thick pulp. Add more water if necessary at any time to prevent the fruit sticking to the bottom of the pan.

3 If you like jam very smooth and more like a purée or paste, pass it through a sieve; otherwise bottle it as it is in warm, dry sterilised jars. Leave it to cool before sealing the jars and store in a cool place. The jam will keep for at least 6 months if unopened.

Elderflower cordial

The shrubby elder (*Sambucus nigra*) is so common in the countryside that it is easy to pass by. Yet in early summer it provides one of the most distinctive ingredients of the preserving year. The heavily scented blossoms make a refreshing cordial (made following a similar method to that for the ginger and lemon cordial on page 122) that you can dilute with still or sparkling mineral water. The fragrance, as well as the taste, evokes lazy summer afternoons. Gather the flower heads on dry, sunny days, away from busy roads, and select flower heads that are fresh and white, avoiding older creamy-yellow blossoms.

20 heads of elderflower

1.5kg sugar

1.2 litres water

40g citric acid

2 lemons, thinly sliced

2 oranges, thinly sliced

Equipment needed

clip-top or corked bottles

Makes about 1.5 litres

1 Shake the flowers, face down, to remove any unwanted insects.

2 Place the sugar and water in a stainless steel or enamel pan and warm slowly, stirring, to dissolve the sugar completely, then bring the resulting syrup to a boil.

3 Add the flowers, return to the boil, then remove from the heat.

4 Add the other ingredients, stir well, then leave, covered, in a cool place for 24 hours.

5 Strain the cooled cordial into clean clip-top or corked bottles and sterilise.

6 This delicious cordial will keep for around 2 months in the refrigerator; if frozen in plastic containers, it will last for a year or more – so be sure to make plenty.

Chapter 5

THE BUTCHER'S

With meat long a much-valued part of our diet, the profession of the butcher is an ancient one that can be traced back to the medieval guilds. For generations, the butcher's shop, with its display of cuts of meat, poultry, sausages and hams, was an important establishment among the high street's parade of shops. Nowadays, the butcher's shop is all too often something of an endangered breed, so if you have a good butcher nearby, do support it.

For hundreds of years, quality meat was a luxury, enjoyed by the wealthy and privileged, with the ability to dine on good meat a sign of high social status in many cultures. A good butcher sources their meat carefully, working closely with the farms and slaughter houses for optimum quality. As well as the issue of animal welfare, there are practical reasons as this means they can keep close control on the rearing, finishing and hanging of the meat. A good butcher will still hang and cut up the animals into the various different cuts and joints of meat.

Meat, a precious, protein-rich food, was not to be wasted, and many of our traditional foods made from meat are ingenious ways of using up every scrap of an animal carcase: blood sausages, such as black pudding or boudin noir; offal-based parcels, such as haggis or faggots; and brawn, made from the pig's head.

Pigs

Of all the livestock raised for meat, the pig offers the widest variety of products and the least waste. From bacon to ham, chitterlings, salami, scratchings, pâtés and pies, virtually every inch is used up in the venerable tradition of nose-to-tail eating – even the pig's fat is rendered to make lard that is invaluable in potting (see page 140) and pastry (see page 38). The pig has always been valued for its ability to forage for its food and to thrive on scraps.

Cattle

Beef is another versatile meat, with the carcase producing a range of cuts, from the cheaper ones, such as fat-rich ox cheeks or oxtail, ideal for slow-braising, to highly regarded, expensive cuts, such as tender, lean steak or rib of beef. The best beef comes from extensively reared grass-fed cattle, slowly matured and hung once slaughtered, with well-marbled beef a good indicator of quality. Traditional breeds of cattle that are bred for beef include the Herefordshire, Chianina and Aberdeen Angus. Veal is the term given to the meat from calves, with rose veal representing a welfare-friendly option.

Sheep

Another domesticated source of meat is the sheep, from which we get lamb, hoggett (overwintered lamb) and mutton (the term given to meat from sheep over one year old). In some countries, lamb is eaten very young, while still at the suckling stage, but it is more usually eaten when weaned, between 4 months and a year.

Poultry

Poultry includes chicken, turkey, duck and goose. The best, and most expensive, is reared to free-range standards, where the birds have unlimited access to the outdoors for exercise and develop at a natural rate. There are various other standards of animal welfare which cover housing and feed, and it follows the more intensively reared the bird, the more inexpensive it will be.

Game

Game animals and birds, such as wild boar, wild deer (venison), grouse, partridge, pigeon, pheasant or wild duck, are noted for their flavour and the leanness of their meat, which are a result of their active outdoor lives. The most important aspects when choosing game are its age, how it has been slaughtered, and the conditions and time for which it has been hung.

Preserving meat

A good butcher or game dealer will know about hanging their meat: a process of ageing or maturing the meat in a controlled, cool, well-ventilated environment. Due to enzyme action in this process, this will both tenderise the meat and game and give it flavour. Drying meat is thought to be the most ancient form of preserving meat.

Salting is a long-practiced way of preserving meat by removing moisture, since salt has a dehydrating effect. We have long valued salt for its flavour and for its preserving qualities, both mining it from the ground and producing it by evaporating seawater. The role of salt as a preservative is explored further in the next chapter (see page 166). Many of our cured meats are made through a complex and time-consuming process, which uses salt as a basis. Today, rather than preserving as a necessity, these products are enjoyed in their own right as luxuries, such as meltingly soft rillettes and the confit of duck, often used to add flavour and succulence to a French cassoulet.

The difference in flavour between a lovingly cured meat product, produced with skill and time, and a mass-produced product, where technology and additives have been used to by-pass the traditional process, is noticeable. These crafts may be threatened, but there are still skilled butchers and artisanal producers committed to creating fine meat products. The home cook looking to work with meat has many examples and recipes to follow, from making sausages and potting meats to slow-cooking pâtés and terrines.

Sausages

Originating from the frugal desire to make use of every precious scrap of meat, the sausage, usually a mixture of finely chopped or ground seasoned meat in a casing, exists in many forms. Although pork is the popular choice of meat for sausages, they can be made from any meat, including beef, lamb and venison, or poultry, such as duck or chicken.

Traditionally, the casings for the chopped meat were made from animal's intestines, used as a natural container for the meat filling, with the long, narrow shape that characterises a classic sausage deriving from the shape of a casing. Another natural wrapping for sausages is caul fat (the lacy, fatty membrane that encases the internal organs), which is used to

wrap around sausage meat patties such as Greece's sheftalia. Although artificial casings (usually made from collagen) are now widely used in the mass-manufacture of sausages, natural or 'fresh' casings made from animal intestines are still the preferred option. Artisanal sausage makers value their slightly porous quality, which allows the sausages to dry gradually or to cook without bursting.

Broadly speaking, sausages can be divided into the three following groups:

Fresh sausages Made from fresh meat, these are raw and have a short shelf life, depending on the quantity of additives. They must be cooked before eating and should be consumed within a few days of making.

Cured sausages Dried or salted sausages, which can be sliced and eaten without cooking, include Italy's salami crudo and France's saucisson sec. In the Mediterranean region, the dry, warm climate enables curing to take place easily.

Cooked or part-cooked sausages These are sausages that are cooked or part-cooked during production. North European countries, such as Poland and Germany, with their cold, wet climates, have a long tradition of making cooked sausages, many of which are also smoked to enhance their flavour and keeping properties.

Left: Paprika gives chorizo sausage its distinctive red colouring
Opposite: Parma ham and salami on offer at Lidgate's

Meet the producer: Lidgate's

A much-respected, well-established butcher's, Lidgate's is a family affair, currently run by David Lidgate, the fourth generation of the family to manage the business. All their meat is meticulously sourced from free-range and organic farms and carefully selected with an eye to quality.

'I vet all the meat that comes into the shop,' explains David, 'and if I don't think it's good enough, I'll send it back. I know by the look and the feel of the carcase whether it's what I want. It's like tasting a wine in a restaurant before you buy it.' This careful sourcing means that their smart shop offers an eye-catching display of meat and meat products, from salt marsh lamb and grass-fed beef to Lidgate's famous pies and home-cured hams.

Sausages, one of their bestsellers, are freshly made by Lidgate's every morning. For David, the quality of the meat he uses is key. 'You can't make a good sausage without good pork,' he declares, 'and by that I mean pork from properly reared, properly fed pigs. All our pork comes from pigs grown in the open air, with access to fields. Some producers are using woodlands to feed their pigs, which is great. The pigs love acorns and beech mast and it not only gives a slightly nutty flavour, but also makes for healthy pigs. Happy pigs make good pork.

'It's not just the quality of our meat that's important to our sausages, it's the quality of everything else that goes in them. Our herbs and spices have to be fresh, because if they're old and stale, they'll lack flavour. Although our sausages are lean, we don't make the leanest sausages because you need some fat in the recipe to give the sausage flavour and succulence. We use around 15-20% of fat, but it must be good fat. I can tell whether the fat is good or not by its colour and feel. We use natural casings because I think they

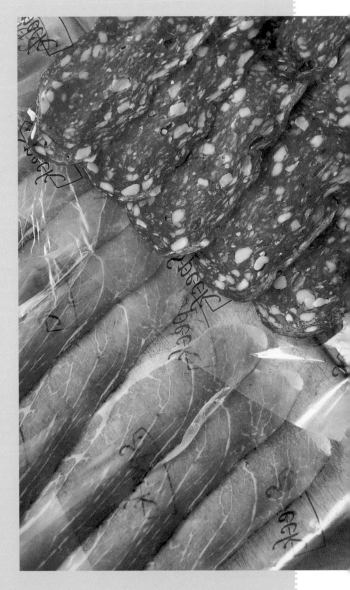

produce a better product. The artificial casings dry out more, especially where the linkage is, and that looks unattractive. Our sausages are displayed loose — not packeted — and they must look good as well as taste good. We taste everything we make, from the pies to our hams. It's not rocket science; it's hard work and liking what you do.'

Fresh sausages

A craft sausage maker will use a high meat content, made with a mixture of fat (to give succulence and flavour) and lean and fatty meat, such as shoulder and leg. An often recommended ratio is between three and four parts meat to one part fat, though sausage makers will tweak this ratio in their own personal recipe. In Western Europe, fresh pork, with its natural high fat content, is the favoured meat for all sausage making, whether fresh, cured or cooked. The meat mixture can then be flavoured, traditionally with herbs such as sage, or garlic or spices such as the sweet or hot paprika used in Spanish chorizo.

To make sausages, the meat mixture is first minced to create sausage meat, a process usually done using a mincer or a food processor. Because mincing heats up the meat, it is recommended that you work with very cold meat straight out of the fridge. The texture of the minced sausage meat can be varied to personal taste, with a very fine mince producing a smooth sausage and a rougher, coarser-cut mince producing a more textured one. This meat mixture is then seasoned and in order to check that you have achieved the right level of seasoning, fry a little piece of the sausage meat mixture until cooked through and taste it. The joy of making your own sausages in small batches is, of course, that you control what goes into them.

Cured sausages

The process of making dry-cured sausages is a time-consuming one. As with fresh sausages, the meat mixture should contain a proportion of fat, but this time in a ratio of one part fat to two or three parts meat, to ensure succulence, with the meat finely diced, minced or pounded to a paste. Hard pork back fat (ask your butcher for this) is often used because of its firm texture. Differences in the texture of the meat mixture are used to create different types of dry-cured sausages, with, for example, France's saucisson de montagne being made with more coarsely minced meat than saucisson de ménage.

The dry-curing process requires dehydration, and so salt is added to the meat to draw out the water from it. A tiny amount of nitrite is also added to inhibit bacterial growth and gives the cured meat a red colour rather than the grey colour naturally produced by the process, with saltpetre (potassium nitrate) traditionally used. In addition, spices and flavourings are added, such as peppercorns in Felino salami, and sometimes alcohol, such as red wine. The mixture is tightly packed into the casings to make sure that there are no pockets of air in which bacteria could thrive, then set aside to dry out for several weeks, usually in a cool, well-ventilated place. Natural casings are favoured for dry-cured sausages as they act as a protective barrier, but allow the meat to 'breathe' and gradually dehydrate. As the sausages dry, they develop a harmless white mould bloom on their surface, an indicator that the maturing is progressing as it should. During the maturing of many types of dry-cured sausages, the lactic-acid bacteria present in the meat set to work, partly fermenting it. This acidic environment, in which bacteria find it hard to exist, then extends these sausages' keeping qualities. The maturing process results in aromatic, intensely flavoured sausages with a firm texture.

Cooked or part-cooked sausages

When it comes to cooked sausages, parboiling, boiling and smoking are the different methods. Italy's large, fine-textured mortadella sausage, made from pork flavoured with peppercorns and pistachios, is steamed or poached. German bratwurst sausages are scalded during the making process and should then be heated before eating. Smoking, which adds a distinctive flavour, is often combined with other processes, such as dry-curing or parboiling.

Opposite: A selection of salami

Hams

Strictly speaking, a ham is the cured back leg of an animal, although the term is often used to include the cured shoulder. Most people think of a ham as coming from a pig, but it can also be used to describe meats such as mutton and venison.

A ham can be dry cured or dry salted, brine cured, or a mixture of the two, hung for weeks, months or even years to mature, then smoked or not, and finally eaten raw or cooked. England's Bradenham ham, for example, is dry cured, then soaked in a brine flavoured with molasses and finally smoked, resulting in a subtle, sweet-flavoured ham, while Wiltshire ham is cured in brine and York ham is dry-cured. Many of the finest hams, such as Italy's Parma ham or Spain's Iberico ham, are dry-cured, produced by an intricate process of salting the meat and setting it aside to cure in cool, airy conditions for

many months. The true Iberico ham is made from a specific breed of pig, Spain's indigenous Iberico (also known as pata negra or the 'black-hoofed' pig), with the best ham coming from pigs which forage for acorns and wild plants in forests. The resulting hams are costly luxuries with a rich, distinctive flavour and texture, classically simply sliced and eaten.

Above: Ham going through the air-drying process

Meet the producer: Trealy Farm

Trealy Farm is noted for their range of around 50 fresh and charcuterie pork products, all carefully produced on the farm itself.

'Our starting point is that we use locally sourced, free-range, traditional breeds of pigs,' declares owner James Swift. 'These are slow-growing breeds that have denser, drier meat that is ideal for charcuterie. These traditional breeds also produce more marbled meat, which you want as you need the fat for flavour, moisture and texture.We want pigs that weigh about 100kg, at which point they're up to a year old.

'These pigs are then seam butchered, that is cut by muscle, so every muscle is taken out. From each muscle we make at least one, sometimes two or three, products,' explains James. 'Different muscles have different qualities. Silverside, for example, is a muscle that does a lot of work, so it's tough. We use that for a Monmouthshire air-dried ham. Chump, another muscle at the end of the loin, is very tender. We use that to make a beech-smoked, air-dried ham, which is much softer and more delicate than the Monmouthshire.'

The process of transforming this pork into sausages and charcuterie is 'very scientific'. 'All our air-dried products are naturally fermented and to do that we need to control the environment every step of the way. Very small differences in the process will affect the flavour.' The type of salt used to dry-cure his products is very important. 'Salts vary in their flavours and action, so you'll find charcuterie producers always source their salt from one particular area or producer; we're currently experimenting with sea salt from Anglesea. We also need nitrites to prevent botulism, so we use organic curing salts with a very low nitrite content, about a fifth of what you'd normally get.'

James is committed to creating his charcuterie products using traditional, time-consuming methods. 'We don't use monosodium glutamate (MSG), as lots of people do. We want to work with natural flavours, so to use MSG seems a bit of a cheat.' The curing period for Trealy Farm's products can be up to 5–6 months for the hams. 'Because we're curing muscles rather than legs, they're smaller pieces of meat, so they don't take so long.' The result of his careful sourcing of the meat and intricate process of curing is an individual range of subtly flavourful charcuterie. For James, it is the fact that he is producing something unique that places him in the great tradition of charcuterie. 'People talk about air-dried ham as though it's one thing, but it's not. There are hundreds of different hams or different chorizos, all of which can vary enormously from each other, depending on how they're made, the breed of pig, the microclimate where they're produced. To me, that's the beauty of charcuterie.'

Pâtés and terrines

Pâtés and terrines are a family of products made from finely minced meat, poultry or fish. The term 'terrine' comes from the French name for a type of lidded, ovenproof dish in which pâtés are cooked and now generally means a kind of pâté with a chunkier texture, often layered.

Classic ingredients for both pâtés and terrines include offal, such as liver, and game. Popular flavourings include onion, garlic, herbs, spices, nuts, fruits, vegetables and – a luxurious touch – truffles with their distinctive characteristics. The mixture is gently baked, sometimes in a bain-marie, and served hot or cold. It can vary in texture, from soft and melting to coarse and firm.

Potted meats and fish

Potting is a traditional way of preserving meat, game, poultry and fish, a process where it is first stirred with melted fat, then sealed with a layer of fat – clarified butter or lard – to keep out the air.

Spices, such as nutmeg or mace, are usually added during the process for flavour. The preserving properties can further be extended by first salting the meat, then by long, slow cooking in the fat to draw out the moisture. The preserving properties can be extended again by making a confit – in fact, similar to potting. First, however, the whole joint of meat or poultry is salted, then cooked very slowly and gently in its own fat. The whole joints or pieces are left to cool, until the fat hardens to provide a protective coating. Sealed, usually in stoneware pots or cans, the confit can be kept safely for months.

Another French-based product is rillettes, made by cooking meat (traditionally pork or goose) extremely slowly in fat until tender, then shredding, pounding or mashing the meat, placing it in containers and topping with a layer of fat. Fish rillettes are often made with oily fish such as eel, salmon or sardine, again cooked very gently in butter, then pounded into a paste. For potting, confit and rillettes it is very important that the ingredients are covered by the fat to prevent decay.

Meet the producer: Baxters Potted Shrimps

Established in 1799, this tiny company, still run by members of the Baxter family, has a proud history of producing potted shrimps, with a Royal Warrant from Her Majesty The Queen as a distinguished sign of approval. With a subtle taste of mace and nutmeg, these pots are a lovingly produced delicacy.

'We use locally caught little brown shrimps straight from Morecambe Bay,' explains Mark Smith, manager of Baxters. 'That's very important, as this stretch of the northwest coast produces a very good quality of shrimp; the reason they're so good is in the handling. The guys we buy the shrimps from are third and fourth generation fisherman; all they've done is fish for shrimp. They go out in small boats with a net, pull the net in, then they go riddling through the catch, that's what they call it, picking through and grading the shrimps by size. They boil the shrimps in seawater on board the fishing boat, then place them in a net and put them in the sea over the side of the boat to cool them. This is the same way they've done it for hundreds of years. They then shell the shrimps, which is really laborious, but hand peeling, rather than using machines to peel, results in shrimps with more flavour.

'These are the shrimps that we buy. We then pick through the shrimps ourselves, picking out any tiny bits of shell that are left. I cook 13kg of peeled shrimps at a time. We call it a "stewing", where we cook them with spices and butter. The spice mixture we use is a family secret, handed down through the generations. I can tell you that we don't use clarified butter, we use the best English butter, the same we've used for years. Once cooked, the shrimps are cooled, chilled, then placed in pots. We use very little butter in our final product; our potted shrimps are 85% shrimp, 15% butter. We put a very thin layer of butter on top to seal them and give them a better shelf life.

'The way we produce our potted shrimps is still the same as it has been all through the years; there's no difference in flavour between what we make now and what we made 50 years ago. Like a good cheese, potted shrimps are best eaten at room temperature when the butter has softened. First you get the small, sweet, tender, moist shrimps, then the tongue-tingling aftertaste of the spices. There are a lot more people making potted shrimps nowadays, but ours are still the best.'

Opposite: A freshly baked baguette is the perfect accompaniment to any pâté or terrine
Right: When making potted meat or fish, add some herbs and peppercorns to the hot butter to increase the depth of flavour

Sourcing the ingredients

Buy your meat carefully from a reputable source, such as a good butcher or farm shop. When buying pork, ideally go for a traditional or rare breed of pig. They are hardy creatures, adept at foraging outdoors, and gain weight slowly, to make for well-marbled meat and a good outer layer of fat. Meat from these breeds of pigs, reared with access to the outdoors, tends to be more fuller flavoured with the level of fat needed to produce good charcuterie.

Salt plays a major part in curing meats. For more information on salt see page 166. Sodium nitrite, which is needed to guard against the risk of botulism, can be hard to get hold of. However, special preserving salts containing sodium nitrite are available to the public, and a quick search online will bring up several specialist mail-order companies.

Natural sausage casings are often recommended for their porous quality. These can be sourced online or via reputable butchers. Before use, they need to be soaked for at least two hours, ideally overnight. For caul fat, which is sold fresh and used to wrap around meat parcels, you also need to find a good butcher.

How to store

Always store your meat and fish products carefully and eat them within the recommended period of consumption. Fresh sausages, for example, should be kept in the refrigerator and eaten within a few days. If they won't be consumed soon, it is best to freeze them, then thaw as required.

While whole dried salamis are a preserved product that can be stored in a cool, dry, well-ventilated place, the reality of centrally heated, well-insulated homes means that it's safer to store them in a refrigerator, loosely wrapped in breathable wrapping. Be sure to keep products designed to be eaten raw, such as salamis, well away from fresh meat, poultry or fish to avoid any risk of cross-contamination.

Left: Salami lightly spiced with fennel seeds
Right: The white coating often found on the outside of salami is mould which helps to protect it from outside elements

Making chorizo sausages

These Spanish-style sausages pack a great tasty kick. Ideally, make them a day ahead to allow the flavours to meld and permeate. The most important thing to consider is the hygiene factor. Ensure that everything you are going to use is clean and the work surfaces are sterilised, and just follow the normal good practices of washing hands and cleaning up as you go. When you first start, you can ask your local butcher to help with the casings and the meat. If you want to go on and experiment with many different sausages, you might like to try more specialised equipment and ingredients.

2 metres sausage casing

1kg pork loin

1kg pork belly

2 tablespoons coarse sea salt

5 garlic cloves, finely chopped

2 tablespoons paprika

2 teaspoons cayenne

1 teaspoon ground cumin

1 teaspoon dried oregano

50ml dry Spanish wine

Equipment needed

food mixer with a mincer and sausage-making attachment

large mixing bowl

Makes 2kg

Note: When you first start to make sausages at home, you will need only the equipment listed above. However, if you are making more than a couple of kilos at a time, you might consider buying an electric mincer with sausage attachments. Alternatively, you can buy your meat pre-minced, although this means you cannot control its texture.

1 Soak your casings in plenty of cold water for a minimum of 2 hours to soften them and to remove the excess salt. Wash them again after soaking. Wash the insides of the casings by running tap water through them, then load onto the tube just before you need them.

2 Make sure that your butcher has trimmed all the rind off the pork. Weigh out the seasonings and meaure out the wine so you are ready to get started as soon as the meat is ready (see step 3).

3 Cut the meat into small chunks about 2.5cm square so it will go through the mincer easily. Cover and place the meat in the refrigerator or freezer for no more than an hour, possibly less. You need the meat to be as near to frozen as possible, but DO NOT actually freeze it or the texture will be like sawdust in the sausage. Put the meat through the mincer using a coarse mincer plate, collecting it in a bowl.

4 Add all the other ingredients and mix well. You will feel the meat start to firm up as you mix it. The more you mix, the firmer the texture will be in the finished sausage, so test-cook small pieces as you go until you find the consistency that suits you. At this stage, you can re-mince with a small-holed plate if you want a finer sausage, or leave it coarse, depending on the texture you require.

5 Change the mincing plate to a sausage filling tube, load on the washed casings and force the meat back through the mincer to fill the skins. Tie a knot at the free end of the sausage casing. Hold the casing between your thumb and forefinger and push the filling down with the plunger. You will need to work by trial and error to get the correct pressure needed to fill the casings and the speed of moving your hand away from the tube. Use your free hand to twist the casings as they reach the desired length. Four or five twists between links are all that are needed. At first you may find they are too thick and can burst, or they may be too thin, like chipolatas, but with practice your sausages will come good. The other thing you may find is that you get air pockets forming in the sausages as a result of not filling the hopper with enough meat. Try to get everything working evenly; speed is not important at this stage. Also, get someone to help the first time you make sausages, as it definitely does make it easier.

6 Wrap the links in baking parchment and leave in the fridge overnight so that the flavours have time to combine and develop. You can then cook them or cut into individual links and store in the refrigerator for up to three days or freeze.

Making game terrine

A game terrine should be made two or three days in advance, so the flavours have plenty of time to mellow and blend. It needs a mixture of game along with ham, pork and pork fat for flavour, moisture and texture. This recipe can also be made with hare, rabbit or venison.

450g wild boar, stripped off
the bone, or other meat

115g ham, diced

115g pork fat, diced

½ teaspoon allspice

pinch of cloves

pinch of nutmeg

3½ tablespoons brandy

3½ tablespoons Madeira

salt and freshly ground pepper

450g belly of pork

1 egg

15g truffle, finely chopped (optional)

350g rashers of streaky bacon

Equipment needed

food processor

terrine dish

Serves 10–12

1 Cut half the wild boar into finger-size strips. Mix the strips in a bowl with the ham, pork fat, allspice, cloves and nutmeg. Pour in the brandy and Madeira, season and stir thoroughly. Cover the bowl and leave to marinate for 1–2 hours.

2 Preheat the oven to 180°C/350°F/ Gas 4. Put the remaining wild boar along with the belly of pork in a food processor and whiz until reduced to pieces about 2.5 cm thick. Strain the liquid from the marinade into this mixture. Break in the egg, add the truffle (if using), salt and pepper and whiz again until reduced to pieces about half the previous size. (Be careful not to over-process or chop it too finely as this will result in a heavy and dense pâté.)

4 Place the terrine in a roasting pan and half fill it with boiling water. Bake in the preheated oven for 1¼–1½ hours. To test to see whether it is ready, remove the greaseproof paper and insert a skewer into the pâté: if the juices that run out are clear, it is cooked. Allow the terrine to cool slightly, then place a plate or a piece of wood on top and weight it with about 90g of weights to press down the terrine. Refrigerate overnight and keep for at least 2 days before serving to allow the flavours to mellow. Keep the terrine well wrapped and refrigerated and it should last for up to 5 days.

3 Line a suitable terrine with the bacon rashers, reserving two or three. Spread one-third of the chopped mixture on the bottom and cover with half of the boar strip mixture. Repeat the process and finish with a final layer of the chopped mixture. Cover the top with the remaining slices of bacon and lay a sheet of greaseproof paper on top.

Making bresaola

This classic Italian air-dried beef is very tasty and well worth the slow nurturing process. Serve it finely sliced as an antipasti or a first course.

Aged until it becomes hard and turns a dark red, almost purple, colour, bresaola can take up to three months to make, depending on the size of the beef you use. It is made from topside and is lean and tender with a sweet, musty smell.

You also need to think about where you can hang your beef so that the temperature is constant at about 12°C (54°F).

1.3kg topside of beef
30g curing salt
30g demerara sugar
5g black pepper
6g fresh rosemary, chopped
6g fresh thyme, chopped
5 juniper berries

Equipment needed
pestle and mortar
plastic container
muslin
butcher's hook

Makes 750g

1 Trim the meat of all external fat and any membrane. Assemble all the cure ingredients, from the salt to the juniper berries.

2 Pound the cure ingredients in a mortar and pestle until fine. Rub half of the spice cure into the meat, making sure to cover it all, including the ends. Put in a plastic container, cover with clingfilm and refrigerate for 7 days, turning the meat every couple of days.

3 Drain any liquid that might be present and rub in the remaining spice cure. Cover with clingfilm and refrigerate for another 7 days.

4 Take the meat from the refrigerator and rinse all the cure off thoroughly. Let it sit at room temperature for a couple of hours on a rack. Tie the whole thing up in a double layer of muslin and insert a butcher's hook into one end. Hang for at least a month at a temperature of about 12°C (54°F). When it is done, it will feel firm to touch, but still have a slight 'give'. As a guide, it should lose around 40% of its original weight. The bresaola will keep in the refrigerator for up to 2 weeks, wrapped in clingfilm.

Making potted ham

This recipe is made using ham, but you can successfully substitute other cooked meats, such as leftover roast meat or poultry, so it is a useful way of using up scraps of meat that might otherwise be discarded.

200g unsalted butter

300g good-quality cured ham, trimmed of any fat and roughly chopped

¼ teaspoon ground mace

½ teaspoon cayenne

Equipment needed

food processor

4 ramekins or other small dishes

Serves 4

1 Preheat the oven to 150°C/300°F/Gas 2. First, clarify the butter. Simply place the butter in a heavy-based saucepan and heat very gently until the butter has totally melted. Skim off any white scum on the surface, then carefully spoon out the yellow clarified butter from the pan into a container, leaving behind the whitish residue of milky solids, which can be discarded. Place the ham in a food processor, together with two-thirds of the clarified butter, the mace and cayenne. Blend until the mixture forms a fine-textured paste.

2 Divide the mixture evenly among the four ramekins and level the surface. Place the filled ramekins in a deep baking tray, pour in hot water so that it comes halfway up the sides of the ramekins and bake for 20 minutes. Remove the ramekins from the oven and allow to cool. Once cool, use the remaining clarified butter to top each potted ham, forming a layer on top, and place in the refrigerator to chill. Before serving, bring the potted hams to room temperature to allow the butter to soften. The potted hams can either be stored in the refrigerator, where they will keep for a few days, or frozen.

Using your produce

Jambon persillé

For this recipe, which is a variation on the terrine on page 146, buy either the knuckle end of gammon or prime hock or gammon slipper. If you buy it on the bone, allow extra for the weight of the bone and make sure you skin it before cooking. As jambon persillé should have quite a meaty – but not too overpowering – flavour, it is a good idea to start off by boiling the joint, throwing away the water and starting again. This way you are certain of getting rid of some of the saltiness. If you do not have a terrine or pie dish, you can always make this in a round bowl. The only disadvantage is that you will not be able to cut it into neat rectangular slices for serving, but if it tastes as good as it should, it is unlikely your guests will mind.

675g piece of gammon (see introduction)

11 black peppercorns

2 bay leaves

1 calf's foot

1 small knuckle of veal

few sprigs of chervil

few sprigs of tarragon

few sprigs of thyme

few sprigs of parsley

450ml dry white wine

2 teaspoons white wine vinegar

large bunch of curly parsley, finely chopped

Equipment needed

terrine or pie dish

Serves 8

1 Put the gammon in a deep saucepan, add just enough water to cover and bring to the boil over a medium heat. Just as the water starts to bubble, remove the pan from the heat, pour off the water and start again. This time add 3 peppercorns and one of the bay leaves and leave the ham to simmer gently for 25 minutes.

2 Lift the gammon out of the water and, when it is cool enough to handle, trim away the fat and cut the meat into sizable chunks.

3 Meanwhile, in a clean saucepan, put the calf's foot, knuckle of veal, the herbs tied together in a bunch and the remaining bay leaf and peppercorns along with about 1 litre of water. Bring to the boil over a low heat, skimming off the fat as it rises. Cover and simmer gently for about 90 minutes, then pour in the wine, add the gammon meat and simmer for a further 30 minutes, or until the meat is very soft.

4 Using a slotted spoon, transfer the gammon to a terrine, pie dish or large bowl and flake it with a fork. Strain the liquid into a bowl through a strainer lined with muslin. Add the vinegar and leave it to set slightly, then stir in the parsley and pour it over the ham. Leave it overnight in a cold place to set and serve turned out on a serving dish and cut into slices. The dish will keep for 3–4 days in the refrigerator.

Parma ham with figs and balsamic dressing

The combination of sweet, salty Parma ham or a local prosciutto crudo – both air-dried meats, like bresaola (see page 149) – and a yielding soft fruit like ripe figs or melon is one of life's little miracles. This is an all-time classic, and none the worse for that. It is quick to assemble, providing you have excellent, thinly sliced ham and perfect, garnet-centred figs.

4 large or 8 small fresh ripe figs (preferably purple ones)

1 tablespoon good balsamic vinegar

extra-virgin olive oil

12 thin slices of Parma ham or prosciutto crudo

150g fresh Parmesan cheese, broken into craggy lumps, to serve

crushed black pepper

Serves 4

1 Take each fig and stand it upright. Using a sharp knife, make two cuts across each fig, not quite quartering it, but keeping it intact. Ease the figs open and brush with balsamic vinegar and extra-virgin olive oil.

2 Arrange three slices of Parma ham on each plate with the figs and Parmesan on top. Sprinkle with more oil and plenty of crushed black pepper.

Pork, fennel and spinach terrine with drunken figs

I love the simplicity of this chunky terrine (see also page 146), made from pork, flavoured with fennel seeds and layered with spinach. Its small size makes it perfect for a small party of guests or to serve for a simple snack or lunch.

2 bay leaves

150g dry-cured streaky bacon

200g spinach, chopped

2 tablespoons olive oil

1 small onion, chopped

1 tablespoon fennel seeds

2 garlic cloves, finely chopped

300g pork belly, coarsely minced

200g lean pork fillet, diced

½ teaspoon ground nutmeg

½ teaspoon ground allspice

1 teaspoon sea salt

½ teaspoon black pepper

slices of crusty bread, to serve

For the drunken figs

20 dried Turkish figs, halved

250ml Marsala wine

Equipment needed

small terrine or loaf tin oiled with rapeseed oil

Serves 6

1 To make the drunken figs, put the figs, Marsala wine and 4 tablespoons of water in a saucepan and bring nearly to boiling point. Remove from the heat, cover and leave to cool.

2 Preheat the oven to 180°C/350°F/Gas 4. Arrange the bay leaves over the bottom of the terrine, then lay the bacon across the width. Put the spinach in a colander and pour over boiling water to blanch. Refresh with cold water, squeeze out any excess water and set aside.

3 Heat the olive oil in a frying pan over a low heat and sauté the onion, fennel seeds and garlic for 10 minutes, or until soft but not yet brown. Transfer to a large bowl with half of the spinach, the pork belly and fillet, nutmeg and allspice. Add the salt and pepper and mix well.

4 Put half of the pork mixture in the prepared terrine and press down firmly. Top with the spinach, then the remaining pork mixture. Press down firmly, then fold over any overhanging bacon. Firmly cover with oiled aluminium foil and put in a baking dish. Fill the baking dish with enough water to come halfway up the sides of the terrine. Bake in the oven for 1 hour. Transfer to a dish to catch any juices and put a weight on top. Leave to cool, then chill overnight or for 1–2 days. Serve with the drunken figs and bread. The terrine will keep for three days in the refrigerator.

Potted cheese

The potting process (see page 140) doesn't have to be restricted to meat, it can be used on other ingredients, too. Almost every traditional cookery book includes at least one recipe for potted cheese and there are hundreds of versions — with or without walnuts, anchovies, cayenne and even sometimes with a pinch of sugar. Here one of Mrs Beeton's recipes has been adapted for modern-day machinery, as the food processor makes it unnecessary to pound by hand in a pestle and mortar.

225g Cheddar cheese
225g butter
large pinch of ground mace
large pinch of mustard powder
large pinch of cayenne
40ml dry sherry

Equipment needed
food processor
Serves 4

1 Put all the ingredients in a food processor and blend until the mixture is smooth.

2 Spoon the mixture into an earthenware jar, cover with greaseproof paper and store in a cool place. It will keep for several weeks, but is ready to be eaten within a couple of days.

Potted salmon

Fish paste, a corrupted form of potted fish, is one of those extraordinary British inventions that, understandably enough, no other country has adopted with any enthusiasm. However, properly done, potted preparations are excellent (see also page 140).

225g poached salmon, boned and cooled
3 anchovy fillets
juice of ½ lemon
285g butter
pinch of mace
pinch of ground ginger
salt and freshly ground black pepper
Serves 4

1 Pound the salmon with the anchovy fillets, lemon juice and 225g of the butter until smooth (this is easier and quicker if done in a food processor). Add the mace and ginger and season to taste.

2 Pack the mixture tightly in a suitable pot. Melt the remaining butter and pour over the fish to seal. The salmon will keep in the refrigerator for up to 5 days.

Sausages with spinach, raisin and pine nuts

Home-made sausages are perfect for this recipe as there is absolutely no point in attempting it unless your pork sausages are meaty, luscious and wrapped in natural skins.

1 tablespoon olive oil

10 good-quality pork sausages

2 large onions, finely sliced

2 garlic cloves, finely sliced

3 tablespoons balsamic vinegar

25g raisins

25g pine nuts

500g fresh baby spinach, washed and drained

sea salt and freshly ground pepper

mashed potatoes, to serve

Serves 3–4

1 Heat the oil in a large, heavy-based frying pan, add the sausages and fry gently for about 3–4 minutes or until the skins just begin to start browning all over. Toss in the onions and garlic and cook gently with the sausages until they begin to soften. Add the balsamic vinegar, raisins and pine nuts and fry gently for a few minutes until the onions and pine nuts start to turn golden.

2 Pile the spinach on top of the sausages, turn down the heat and, stirring continuously, wait until it has collapsed and wilted. Turn the heat up again and simmer until most of the liquid from the spinach has evaporated and the sauce is, once again, syrupy. Season and serve the sausages with the sauce spooned over a bowl of mashed potato.

Skinless sausages

Making your own sausages really is even easier when you avoid the time consuming part of stuffing them into skins (see page 144). How, you are probably wondering, do they hold together? Very simply, the meat is chopped in a food processor, kneaded lightly with the hands and rolled into sausage shapes, which are wrapped in kitchen foil and lightly poached before being grilled or fried.

450g lean belly or shoulder of pork

115g hard-back fat

1 garlic clove

bunch of flat-leaf parsley

large pinch of sea salt

small pinch of ground cloves

small pinch of ground ginger

small pinch of ground nutmeg

30g fresh breadcrumbs

freshly ground black pepper

Equipment needed

food processor

foil and string

Makes 6

1 Roughly cut the pork and fat into pieces of a size that the food processor can handle. Put them in the food processor with the garlic, parsley, sea salt, cloves, ginger, nutmeg, breadcrumbs and a generous amount of black pepper. Whiz until all the ingredients are mixed together and reduced to the texture of reasonably coarse breadcrumbs. You do not want to over-process the meat or this will make the sausage far too dense; on the other hand, if you do not process them enough, they will not hold together.

2 Tip the meat out into a bowl and divide it into six portions, each weighing 85–115g. Using your fingers, knead the mixture lightly to make sure it sticks together, then roll it out between the palms into a sausage shape about 10cm long. Wrap each sausage in a piece of foil and secure each end by twisting the foil tightly and tying it with string.

3 Have ready a large saucepan filled with gently simmering water, drop in the sausages and simmer them for about 10 minutes. Using a slotted spoon, lift them out and put them in a colander. As soon as they are cool enough to handle, unwrap them and leave to drain.

4 Finish by browning them: either by brushing them lightly with olive oil and grilling them under a preheated grill, or by frying them in a little olive oil or butter over a moderate heat. Serve with onion marmalade.

Smoky sausage and bean casserole

The Italians use a mixture of onions, carrots and celery sautéed in olive oil as the base for many classic soups and casseroles. This holy trinity of veggies is called a soffritto and works well here in a hearty sausage stew.

1 tablespoon light olive oil

12 chipolata sausages

1 garlic clove, chopped

1 leek, thinly sliced

1 carrot, diced

1 celery stick, diced

400g tinned chopped tomatoes

1 teaspoon Spanish smoked paprika

2 tablespoons maple syrup

2 sprigs of fresh thyme

400g tinned cannellini beans, drained and rinsed

toasted sourdough bread, to serve

Serves 4

1 Heat the oil in a heavy-based saucepan over high heat. Add the sausages in two batches and cook them for 4–5 minutes, turning often until cooked and an even brown all over. Remove from the pan and set aside.

2 Add the garlic, leek, carrot and celery and cook for 5 minutes, stirring often. Add the tomatoes, paprika, maple syrup, thyme, beans and 500ml water and return the sausages to the pan.

3 Bring to the boil, then reduce the heat to medium and simmer for 40–45 minutes, until the sauce has thickened.

4 Put a slice of toasted sourdough bread on each serving plate, spoon the casserole over the top and serve.

Chapter 6

THE SMOKEHOUSE

Smoking food in order to enhance its keeping qualities is an ancient practice, the origins of which are lost in time. Certainly it is very easy to imagine that hunters or fishermen seeking to dry their catch near a fire noticed the effect that the smoke had on the food, both flavouring it, drying it, colouring it and enabling it to stay safely edible for longer.

Early smoking

Smoking can be carried out over an open fire out of doors or in a more controlled enclosed space. Originally, foods would have been smoked simply by hanging them above the household hearth or in the chimney. However, given that smoking over an open fire in a house carries the risk of the home burning down, it led to the construction of purpose-built smokehouses, narrow, high buildings in which the food could be hung above the smoke as it rose to the top of the building.

As preservation was the motivating factor, smoking food could take several months, which would – in pre-refrigeration days – substantially lengthen its shelf life. Herrings, an important food for the poor, might be smoked for several weeks, resulting in 'red herrings', with the fish highly colored by the fire. The refinement of first curing, either with a dry or brine cure, developed as did two distinct methods of smoking. Hot-smoking, where the food comes in close proximity with both the heat source and the smoke, and cold-smoking, where the food is exposed to the smoke but kept at a distance from the heat.

Developments in smoking

Two nineteenth-century developments – the railways and refrigeration – impacted hugely on our food. The need to preserve was no longer a priority and smoking developed as a means of enhancing flavour. The kipper, a cold-smoked herring that is a classic British breakfast food, is an example of this trend. Another is smoked salmon, which came about due to the Jewish diaspora from Eastern Europe to London and New York.

The twentieth century saw the development of the mechanical kiln, powered by electricity. In-built thermostats enabled the internal temperature to be controlled and set as required. This largely, though not entirely, displaced those century-old traditional smokehouses.

Modern short cuts

The industrialisation of smoking foods has seen various short cuts developed to speed up what is, by its nature, a slow, time-consuming process. One such method used to speed up the curing process before smoking is by injecting the food with brine rather than dry-curing it with salt or immersing it in brine – a practice deplored by artisanal curers. Both curing and smoking are processes that dehydrate food, causing loss of weight. Cynical industrial practice, however, now sees the addition of water-retentive phosphates to brine cure solutions, meaning that the food ends up weighing more. In addition, liquid smoke, made by passing smoke through water, is used to flavour foods rather than by the process of actually smoking them.

Artisanal smokers

Smoking is a way of changing and enhancing the flavour of food, and thankfully, there are still artisanal producers committed to smoking food using traditional skills and methods, from dry-curing to cold-smoking. The flavour of smoked foods skilfully made with time and care is far superior to those produced using short-cut techniques, making them foods to be savoured and enjoyed.

Right: Pork products such as hams and salamis greatly benefit from the processes of smoking and curing

Fuels for smoking

The fire used for smoking is mostly wood based as not only does it give flavour, but is, and always has been, widely available.

Phenolic compounds in wood smoke delay the onset of rancidity, to which fat is prone. Hence smoking is often used to preserve fat-rich foods (such as cheese, bacon or oily fish, such as herrings or eels), as well as non-fatty foods (such as game). As softwoods give an overly resinous flavour to the food being smoked, hardwoods, such as oak, beech or birch, are best for smoking. These woods each impart a specific flavour to the food being smoked, with hickory being the favoured wood for smoking in the USA. It is important to be sure that the wood you are using has not been chemically treated, as this would result in unhealthy residues on the food. Aromatics such as apple wood or herbs are also used as fuel to enhance the flavour of the food. Wood used for smoking is available in a variety of different forms, including sawdust, briquettes made from compressed sawdust, wood pellets, shavings, chips and chunks.

Other fuel sources for food smoking include peat (though, of course, this is a controversial fuel because of its environmental implications), grapevine clippings and dried seaweed, with all of these sometimes used in addition to wood as aromatics.

Hot-smoking

Hot-smoking is a process where the food is placed close to the heat source, so that it cooks at the same time as it is smoked, usually at a temperature of 55–80°C (131–176°F). Since it cooks the food, hot-smoking creates a firm, dry texture. It can be done at home simply using a covered container, such as a casserole or wok, lined with foil, with the 'fuel' consisting of rice or aromatics such as tea leaves or spices.

Above: The ideal wood for smoking is hard and free from sap
Opposite: Smoked fish seasoned with pepper

Meet the producer: Black Mountains Smokery

Run by husband-and-wife team Jonathan and Joanna Carthew, this smokery is noted for the range and quality of its smoked foods.

'The quality of what we start with is important,' declares Joanna. 'If you start with a rotten product and smoke it, it will still be rotten. We do a lot of commissioned smoking for fishermen, and they often try to give us the less-good fish, but we point out that the really fresh, prime fish will smoke really well. The sourcing is very important to us. We buy farmed fish, not wild, on principle from a reputable fish farm and we don't smoke fish on a Monday because then you're smoking fish that's sat around all weekend. Our ducks come from Gressingham because we want to support British agriculture; they have a good meat content, not too fat, and a great gamey flavour.'

Transforming these raw ingredients into smoked foods involves dry-curing and brining, both using sea salt. 'Generally, we dry-cure for cold-smoking and brine for hot-smoking,' explains Joanna. 'Our house style is a delicate one, which is created both by using a light brine and by not over-smoking. In the old days, smoking was a way of preserving the food, so it was very smoky, very salty in order to keep it safely; we don't need to do that nowadays. Our hot-smoked salmon is mild and our duck breast is very balanced. We don't want to just taste the smoke and the tannins; we want the flavour of the food to come through too.

'We use modern kilns, which work on the same principle as traditional ones, but have the advantage of having a fan so that the smoke is evenly circulated; in the old ones, you had to keep moving the food from the top to the bottom to get an even smoke. We always use oak, which is traditional; we have a good local source of oak. You should always use hardwoods when smoking, not soft woods, otherwise the food would taste like a bubble bath because of all the resin. Our duck breasts are brined for about an hour, cold-smoked for a short time to take away some of the moisture and enhance the smoky flavour, then hot-smoked. You have to keep an eye on everything during the smoking process. We do go home smelling like kippers!'

Cold-smoking

Cold-smoking is a process that takes place below 32°C (90°F), with the food remaining unheated and simply exposed to the smoke. This slowly and gradually affects the flavour of the food, with the interior texture little changed. Possibly the best-known example of a cold-smoked food is smoked salmon.

Cold-smoking is a longer process than hot-smoking, so requires a greater degree of patience. All craft smokers agree that cold-smoking is a more complex process because of the need to keep a steady source of smoke that is enough to cure the food, but at the correct temperature. Furthermore, as constructing a home-made cold smoker to separate the smoke from the direct heat source requires a fair amount of ingenuity, the simplest way for the would-be cold-smoker to practise this craft is to buy a purpose-built home smoker.

The time taken for both hot- and cold-smoking varies according to the size, weight and thickness of the food. The humidity in the atmosphere is another factor to take into account, as smoking on a humid day would take longer due to the moisture in the atmosphere. It can also be tricky to cold-smoke in very hot weather as the heat means that the food will start to cook, which in turn creates a seal that prevents the smoke being absorbed and water extracted.

Above: The simple combination of smoked salmon and cream cheese is a classic
Right: Fillets of smoked fish

Meet the producer: Richardson's Smokehouse

Based in his grandfather's old smokehouse, where he works seven days a week, Steve Richardson creates a wide range of smoked foods, from trout to game birds, such as pigeon, using just sea salt and smoke from oak logs, hand-chopped by Steve.

'We've got one smokehouse, divided into two,' says Steve, matter-of-factly. 'We do the hot-smoking on one side, where we cook the food, and the smoke goes through a vent into the other side, where we cold-smoke it.'

Steve works with both sides of his smokehouse to produce results. The kippers are made from herrings – gutted, brined for two hours in a sea-salt solution, then cold-smoked overnight. 'Cold-smoking is how you make kippers.' The following morning, Steve puts them on trays and they are briefly placed in the hot side of the smokehouse until they take on the level of rich, golden colour that Steve wants. 'Placing them on the tray means that they keep their oil inside,' explains Steve. 'When you cook my kippers you don't need any butter; they've got enough oil inside.' The mackerel at Richardson's is hot-smoked overnight, though again, Steve's intricate knowledge of his smokehouse comes into play. 'I shut the fire down, so it's a very low heat, then the next morning I come in and open the fire up.' The trick is to increase the temperature gradually, not too quickly, as otherwise the mackerel would 'split'. Once Steve thinks the mackerel are cooked, he probes them to check they have reached 75°C (167°F) inside, 'That way, I know they're done; it's a 14–16 hour process.' Different foods are smoked for different periods of time, with his smoked cheeses – a mature English Cheddar and Long Clawson Stilton – cold-smoked at the shelf at the top of the kiln for six days, while haddock fillets (brined for half an hour) are cold-smoked for 16–18 hours. 'We do our smoking the traditional way, the way my grandfather did it,' declares Steve. 'It takes a long while, I admit, but it's the way fish has always been smoked, and it tastes all the better for it.'

Curing with salt

Salt (sodium chloride) is an edible mineral with notable preserving properties. A preliminary curing with salt, either in crystal or brine form, is a key stage of the smoking process. Salt operates through osmosis, penetrating the food and drawing out moisture. You may have seen this effect for yourself when sprinkling salt over sliced cucumber or aubergine — a process that draws the water content from inside these vegetables to the surface.

Salt is either rock salt (salt deposits from within the ground, primarily mined by pumping water into the salt mine to dissolve the salt, then evaporating the resulting brine to create salt crystals) or sea salt, which is obtained by evaporating sea water. The size of the salt crystals depends on the evaporation process. If the brine is rapidly evaporated in a covered container, the salt forms small, fine crystals. If, however, evaporation takes place more slowly and in an open container, then the salt crystallises to form larger fragile flakes. The most highly prized sea salts are those that are created by natural evaporation in shallow, open-air basins

through the heat of the sun, a process used particularly in the Mediterranean region. In France, the layer of white crystals that rise to the top of these basins is known as fleur de sel, 'flower of salt'.

When curing, you can use special preserving salts that contain sodium nitrate. These are available through specialist or online companies. Saltpetre, once a key ingredient for curing, can also be bought from such companies. There are various flavoured salts also on sale, or you can make your own by adding various ground herbs (rosemary or thyme),

or spice (vanilla or chilli), or even sugar. Ironically, one of the newest 'must-have' ingredients is smoked salt, where the salt has been smoked to impart a smokey flavour, and works well with mashed potato.

Dry-curing

This process involves coating the food with salt, by rubbing it in or by burying it in salt and leaving it to stand. Because salt corrodes metal, using ceramic or glass containers is advised. It is a good idea to weight down the food, so it is pressed into the salt.

Care has to be taken not to over-salt the food and the quantity of salt should vary according to the thickness of the food being salted. The thin, tail end of a whole fish, for example, needs less salt sprinkled over it than thicker parts. Depending on how long the dry-curing stage takes, the liquid extracted by the salt must be drained at regular intervals and fresh, dry salt added as required.

The longer the period of dry-curing, the saltier the food and the longer its shelf life. Salt cod, for example, is dry-cured for a period of up to 15 days, with the resulting dried fish so intensely salty that it requires extensive soaking before cooking. If you are going on to smoke your food, the dry-curing stage is much shorter, ranging from one hour to 24.

Extra flavourings can be added to the dry-cure stage by either using a flavoured salt or sprinkling over sugar, herbs or spices, either whole or ground. When cold-smoking fresh wild fish, some craft smokers prefer to freeze the fish first for 48 hours in order to kill off any parasites. Dry-curing must be done in a cool place.

Left: Experiment with different varieties of salt and note the effect each one has on flavour
Right: Smoked salmon

Meet the producer: Cley Smokehouse

Fish and seafood are the stars of the show at this Norfolk coastal smokery, owned and run by Glen Weston, fisherman turned smoker.

'We always use prime fish,' says Glen. 'We're predominantly a shellfish coast here, so we take full advantage of that. Our smoked prawns are one of our best-selling lines.' Glen's smoking kit consists of two traditional cold-smoking chimneys and a separate mini kiln, used for both hot- and cold-smoking, always over oak.

'We don't brine for very long and we don't smoke for very long,' explains Glen, 'so all our smoked fish has a very subtle flavour. I use a weak brine — about 65% salt content — for all my wet-brining. It's important to brine as it gives the fish a glaze.' Cley Smokehouse is particularly noted for its traditional smoked fish, such as buckling (hot-smoked herrings with their heads removed and their roes inside) and kippers. 'The kippers are brined for 15 minutes, placed on tenters (racks) straight away, dried for half an hour, then cold-smoked for 5–6 hours overnight. I come in in the morning and judge whether they're ready or not. To get the desired effect when cold-smoking, you want to smoke for as slowly as possible for as long as possible. We could smoke kippers in three hours, but they'd dry out and get a harsh flavour. When you cold-smoke haddock, it really dries out if you overdo it; of all the fish we do, it needs to be smoked really gently.

'There's no thermostat in my chimneys,' laughs Glen. 'I go by touch and sight. Cold-smoking is not an exact science; it's a very subtle process. The weather affects the smoking process. In summer, when it's hotter, it takes longer to cold-smoke so we leave the fish in the brine a little longer than in the winter to increase the keeping properties of the salt. Every smokehouse has its own style, its own way of doing things, and their smoked foods taste different from each other. What gives me the most satisfaction — makes all the hard work worthwhile — is when someone comes into the shop and says, "Your kipper was the best kipper I've ever tasted."'

Brine-curing

Brine-curing involves immersing the food in brine, which is a mixture of salt and water. It is important that the brine solution is strong or salty enough to preserve effectively. Recommended ratios of salt to water are 200–250g of salt for every litre of water. The salt must be thoroughly dissolved, and to speed up the process use warm or hot water, although it is important to cool the brine down thoroughly before any food is immersed in it. As with dry-salting, it is important to avoid metal containers because of the risk of salt corrosion, and the brining should take place in a refrigerator or cool place.

The brining period depends on the thickness of what is being brined and the desired flavour. The food should be submerged and the brine stirred regularly during the brining period to distribute the salt evenly. Because brine-curing is a quicker way of curing than dry-curing and penetrates the food faster, it is traditionally used for larger cuts of meat, such as whole joints. Flavours can be added to brines by using alcohol, such as cider, wine or beer, as part of the liquid content of the brine mixture, or spices, herbs and flavourings such as sugar.

Preparation for smoking

Once cured, the food is rinsed, patted dry and set aside to 'season', ideally in well-ventilated conditions. This process allows the protein drawn to the surface to form a natural glaze known as a pellicule. This pellicule forms a protective surface over the food to which the smoke can adhere. Once dried, the cured food is then either hot-smoked or cold-smoked.

Home smoking

The smoking process offers the home smoker many opportunities for experimentation. Do bear in mind that for succulent results, it is advisable to choose a naturally fatty or oil-rich food.

Having cured your food, you can then choose whether to cold-smoke or to hot-smoke. Foods that have been already cooked, such as cooked prawns, do not need curing in this way and can simply be smoked. Whichever process you choose, take care to avoid over-curing and over-smoking.

Right: A basic set up for smoking salmon in the home

Sourcing the ingredients

For the best results, experienced smokers recommend using fresh, good-quality ingredients such as prime fish or poultry for the smoking process. Don't be tempted to think that the smoking process will mask the shortcomings of a second-rate ingredient.

Above: Sea salt and pepper
Opposite: Gravlax – cured salmon that is popular in Nordic countries

While good ingredients are a basic starting point, it is worth building up your expertise in smoking first using affordable ingredients, such as mackerel, herring or trout, before experimenting on costly ingredients, such as wild salmon or game.

In choosing which salt to use for curing, purity is an important factor to bear in mind. The process by which sea salt is produced and refined commercially ensures the removal of the bitter minerals otherwise found in sea salt. Coarse sea salt crystals are often used in dry-curing. Unrefined sea salt, characteristically grey in colour, is coated in minerals such as magnesium chloride and sulphate and has a more complex flavour than refined salt. The fine table salt used as an everyday condiment usually contains anti-caking agents, most of which do not dissolve as quickly as salt, so can cause a cloudy brine.

How to store

While curing and smoking have their preserving qualities, it is important to refrigerate your own-smoked food and eat it within a few days of smoking. If you plan to keep smoked food for longer than a few days, then you should freeze it. One of the joys of smoking foods yourself is that freshly smoked food has a wonderful flavour, best enjoyed fresh from the smoker.

Special equipment

The internet is the simplest and best way to track down specialised smoking equipment, such as an electric home smoker or smoking bags (sealable, wood-filled bags designed for use in the home oven).

Making hot-smoked salmon

Hot-smoking salmon gives it a wonderful rich colour and a great smoky flavour. You can serve the salmon either hot or cold. To hot-smoke, you can use a vegetable steamer or a roasting tray with a wire rack and kitchen foil. Using an old vegetable steamer is good because it can be used on top of the stove, the top pan (the steam bit with the holes) will be big enough to capture all the smoke and you can check it's all OK just by lifting the lid. Whilst this technique is quite easy to do at home or in the garden, do be aware that, as the name suggests, hot-smoking does become quite smoky. If you have a sensitive smoke alarm, rig up a hob in the garden instead, or even use your barbecue as an impromptu outdoor smoker.

2 fresh salmon steaks

salt and pepper

2 handfuls of oak chips

lemon rind

fresh thyme

Equipment needed

old vegetable steamer or a roasting tray with a rack and aluminium foil

Serves 2

1 Season the salmon steaks with salt and pepper and place back in the refrigerator while you prepare your smoker.

2 Place the wood chips in the bottom of the steamer pan or roasting tray with the lemon rind and thyme, and place on a high heat until they are hot and smoking (this takes about 10 minutes).

3 Place the salmon in the top part of the steamer or on the wire rack, if using, cover with the lid or foil and leave over the heat for six minutes.

4 Turn off the heat, but leave the lid or foil on and the salmon still over the oak chips for a further 20 minutes so that the smoke can infuse the salmon. The salmon can be served hot or cold.

Making cold-smoked bacon

Cold-smoking is more difficult than hot and needs a more complex gadget or a purpose-built smoke box with a thermostat. Consider using a barbecue with a hose about 3 metres long, a large metal drum, kitchen foil and a meat temperature probe, just to ensure you can control the temperature. The key to cold-smoking is keeping the heat away from the food. You don't want to cook it, just to funnel the smoke so you can impart the flavour. Ideally, you want your temperature in the smoke chamber to be at about 20°C–25°C (68°–77°F).

1kg home-cured bacon (see page 177)

Equipment needed
your smoking box or homemade gadget

Serves 4

1 First, you need to get the wood chips smoking. If you're doing it on a barbecue, use charcoal as your heat source. As the coals turn white, place wood chips on kitchen foil on the cooking rack above them to make the smoke. It's best to soak the wood chips so they smoke for longer. It is useful to keep a water spray nearby so you can damp them down should the temperature rise too high.

2 Then attach a hose from the barbecue vent. Place your cured bacon in the metal drum on a rack covered with foil. Make a hole in the foil and add the hose to the drum, ensuring the drum is completely sealed so the smoke remains inside. Add a temperature probe, if you have one, so you can control the temperature. Smoking is down to personal taste as well as the wood and size of meat, but two hours is a rough guide. Store the bacon in an air-tight container in the refrigerator and it should last up to a week.

Making home-cured bacon

Curing your own bacon is both straightforward and satisfying. The cured bacon can then be cooked as it is or smoked to taste, if desired.

35g rock salt

40g curing salt

10g demerara sugar

1kg pork loin

Equipment needed

non-corrosive container

muslin

Makes 1kg

1 Assemble the salts and sugar to make the cure.

2 Combine the cure ingredients, then rub the cure into both sides of the pork. If you have the rind still on or thick parts of the loin, pierce the rind with a skewer to ensure that the cure penetrates into the meat.

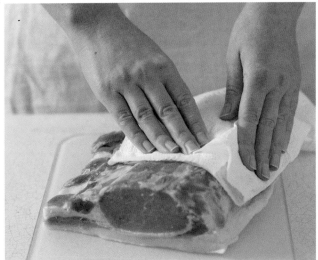

3 Place the pork in a non-corrosive container for 1 week and leave, covered with clingfilm, in the bottom of the fridge or a cold cellar. When the time is up, wipe the loin clean and dry it thoroughly with kitchen paper or muslin. Wrap it in muslin to protect it and hang for 2 to 3 weeks (the longer the better) in a cold pantry or in the fridge. After hanging, the bacon is ready to cook or you can then smoke it (see page 174).

Making brine-cured pork belly

The simple step of brine-curing the pork before roasting it makes it both very tender and flavourful.

1 First, make the brine by bringing the curing salt to the boil in the water. Once boiled, leave it to cool. When it has cooled, transfer the liquor to a plastic or ceramic container and add the pork, making sure it is completely covered with the liquor. The pork can be left for 1–7 days at the bottom of the refrigerator, depending on the time you have. You will get better results the longer you leave it. When it comes out of the brine, you will need to soak it again overnight in fresh water. Once it has been soaked again, prepare it for roasting by drying it thoroughly with muslin or kitchen paper, then leaving it to air dry in the kitchen for an hour.

180g curing salt

1 litre water

1kg pork belly, off the bone

4 cloves

1 teaspoon fennel leaves

8 sage leaves

1 teaspoon fresh rosemary leaves

3 garlic cloves

1 tablespoon olive oil

Equipment needed

plastic or ceramic container

pestle and mortar

Serves 4

2 Preheat the oven to 180°C/350°F/ Gas 4. Mix the rest of the ingredients using a pestle and mortar.

3 Rub the mixture over the pork, then roast for 2 hours. Allow 30 minutes to rest before serving.

Using your produce

Tartare of salmon with cucumber salad

This recipe, adapted from Raymond Blanc's magical book *Recipes from Le Manoir aux Quat'Saisons*, involves dry-curing (see page 167). He stipulates wild salmon, but I think that because it is marinated, this is a bit of an extravagance. As fillet of salmon is essential for this recipe, and as it is also easier to make if you have a matching pair to lay one on top of the other, I suggest buying a whole tail and asking the fishmonger to fillet and skin it for you.

450g farmed salmon tail piece, filleted and skinned

1½ tablespoons chopped fresh dill

zest and juice of 1 lemon

1 tablespoon caster sugar

sea salt and freshly ground white pepper

½ teaspoon Dijon mustard

3 tablespoons sour cream

For the cucumber salad

½ cucumber

sea salt and freshly ground white pepper

1 teaspoon white wine vinegar

2 tablespoons safflower oil

8 sprigs of dill

Equipment needed

tweezers

Serves 8

1 Remove any stray pin bones from the salmon with a pair of tweezers, then lay the fillets flat on a plate. Mix 1 tablespoon of the dill together with the lemon zest, sugar and about 1 tablespoon of salt and rub the mixture over both sides of the salmon. Place one fillet on top of the other, cover with foil and leave to marinate in the refrigerator for 12 hours.

2 At the end of this time, unwrap the salmon and rinse it under cold running water to remove the salt. Drain it well, pat dry with kitchen paper and cut it into thin strips, about 2.5cm long.

3 In a large bowl, mix the lemon juice with the mustard, 2 teaspoons of the sour cream, the remaining dill and a little pepper and stir in the salmon. Leave in a cool place for 1 hour.

4 Meanwhile, prepare the cucumber by cutting it in half lengthwise and scooping out the seeds with a teaspoon. Slice it finely, put in a colander, sprinkle over about 1 teaspoon of salt and let it stand for 30 minutes. Then rinse under cold running water, drain and pat dry. Put the cucumber slices in a small bowl, add the vinegar, oil and a little pepper and mix thoroughly.

5 Raymond Blanc serves the salmon stunningly presented in individual moulds: very effective but surprisingly simple. Using a 5cm pastry cutter as a mould, place it in the centre of a plate and fill it almost up to the top with the salmon, pressing down gently with the back of a teaspoon to pack the fish firmly. Spread 1 teaspoon of sour cream on the top, smoothing it with a spatula, then carefully lift off the pastry cutter. Arrange slices of cucumber around the base and decorate the top with a sprig of dill. Serve with slices of toasted brioche.

Classic gravadlax

Gravlax is a classic Swedish dish of raw marinated salmon flavoured with dill, prepared using a dry cure (see page 167). In pre-refrigerator days, the salmon package would be buried in the cold ground to mature. These days, it is fashionable to cure gravlax for a shorter time, but it gains more flavour and a firmer texture if left for 48 hours.

2 fillets of fresh salmon, 450g each, skin on

50g sugar

100g coarse sea salt

2 tablespoons black peppercorns, crushed

1 large bunch of fresh dill

For the gravlaxsas (gravlax sauce)

60g Dijon mustard

1 teaspoon dried English mustard

3 tablespoons caster sugar

2 tablespoons white wine vinegar

3 tablespoons sunflower oil

3 tablespoons light olive oil

3 tablespoons chopped fresh dill

Equipment needed:

tweezers

Serves 12

1 Using tweezers, remove any remaining bones from the salmon, then put one fillet, skin side down, on a large, double sheet of clingfilm. Mix the sugar, salt, and crushed peppercorns in a bowl, then spread evenly over the flesh. Sprinkle the dill over the top. Arrange the other fillet on top to form a sandwich and wrap up tightly in the clingfilm. Transfer to a non-metal dish and put a small tray and a 450g weight, such as a can of food, on top. Refrigerate for 48 hours, turning over every 12 hours. The salmon will then be ready to eat, but the longer it sits in the marinade, the stronger the flavour will be.

2 To make the gravlaxsas, mix the mustards, sugar and vinegar in a bowl. Slowly beat in the oils as if making mayonnaise, until the sauce is thick. Stir in the dill and refrigerate until needed (you may need to beat it again before serving).

3 Unwrap the fish, reserving the juices, and scrape off the excess peppercorns and herbs. Slice the salmon vertically towards the skin, about 5mm thick, then slice close to the skin horizontally to release the slice. Serve on rye bread with slices of pickled cucumber and the gravlaxsas.

4 Gravlax keeps well wrapped in the refrigerator for at least 3 days. Slice the salmon as you need it, keeping it with the juices and tightly wrapping after each use. Foil tends to pit with the corrosive salt, so use clingfilm.

Variation:

Horseradish and juniper pickled salmon

Finely grate the rind of 2 lemons and put in a bowl with 20 crushed juniper berries, 2 tablespoons sugar, 100g coarse sea salt, 2 tablespoons white peppercorns, crushed, and about 125ml gin. Wrap and chill as in the main recipe. To serve, mix 2 tablespoons horseradish sauce or creamed horseradish with the grated rind of 1 lemon. Slice the fish as in the previous recipe and serve on thinly sliced rye bread or pumpernickel with the sauce.

Kedgeree

Kedgeree is only worth making with quality smoked haddock. Those brash yellow fillets just will not do. Once poached, it flakes easily into satisfying chunks and holds together well when mixed into the rice.

225g smoked haddock

1 small onion, sliced

3 black peppercorns

bay leaf

300ml milk

225g rice

115g butter, melted

3 tablespoons double cream

3 hard-boiled eggs, chopped

3 tablespoons finely chopped curly parsley

salt and freshly ground black pepper

cayenne pepper

Serves 6

1 Put the haddock in a saucepan along with the onion, peppercorns, bay leaf and milk. Place over a medium heat and bring almost to the boil. Turn down the heat and simmer gently for about 5–7 minutes, until the fish is cooked. Drain the fish, discarding the onion, bay leaf and peppercorns. Reserve the milk and leave the fish to cool. Meanwhile, boil the rice in salted water and drain thoroughly.

2 When the fish is cool enough to handle, remove the skin and any bones and flake it gently into sizable chunks by hand; do not be too rough or break the fish down into too small pieces as it will disintegrate when you stir it into the rice.

3 In a clean pan, melt the butter over a medium heat, add the cream, a couple of tablespoons of the reserved milk and the rice and stir until it is thoroughly coated with the mixture. Carefully fold in the flaked fish, the hard-boiled eggs and parsley and cook over a low heat for 1 minute. Adjust the seasoning and serve sprinkled with cayenne pepper.

Salted duck

Recipes for salt duck date back to the nineteenth century. The Chinese have a similar recipe where a mixture of salt and 5-spice powder is used, but my favourite version comes from Denmark, where they salt the duck and marinate it in honey. The result of this dry-curing (see also page 167) is a pungent duck, soft as butter, which literally falls away from its carcase.

1 plump fresh duck, weighing approximately 2kg

115g rock salt

10g saltpetre (available from a chemist or online)

For the marinade

4 tablespoons honey

1.75 litres water

5 bay leaves

8 juniper berries, crushed

1 onion, stuck with cloves

1 carrot, finely sliced

250ml wine vinegar

Serves 4

1 Wipe the duck with a kitchen towel, then, using a sharp knife, make deep incisions all over its skin. Mix the rock salt and saltpetre together and rub it all over the duck, both inside and out, cramming it into the incisions.

2 Meanwhile, melt the honey in the water in a casserole dish, and, when it is dissolved, add the bay leaves, juniper berries, onion and carrot. Simmer the marinade for about 5 minutes, then remove it from the heat and add the wine vinegar. Leave to cool before submerging the duck in the liquid. Leave the duck to marinate for about 3–4 days in a cool place, making sure that it is completely covered in liquid.

3 Drain the duck, carefully skin it and remove the outer loose fat. This should only be done just before cooking, otherwise the flesh will harden. Either return the duck to the marinade (which gives it a sharper, saltier flavour) or place it in a casserole filled with fresh water. Bring to the boil and cook over a low heat or bake it in a slow oven at 150°C/300°F/Gas 2 for about 2 hours. Serve either hot or cold with rice.

Mackerel and bulghur wheat salad

The creamy horseradish dressing in this recipe is a fabulous complement to the richness of the smoked mackerel, while the raw vegetables add crunch and colour. If you wish, you can use couscous instead of bulghur wheat.

60g bulghur wheat

1 tablespoon freshly squeezed lemon juice

1 tablespoon finely snipped fresh chives

½ yellow pepper, deseeded and diced

8 radishes, sliced

75g spinach leaves

150g smoked mackerel fillets, flaked

For the dressing

3 tablespoons fromage frais

2 teaspoons horseradish sauce

1 teaspoon finely snipped fresh chives

freshly ground black pepper, to serve

Serves 2

1 Cook the bulghur wheat in a saucepan of lightly salted boiling water for 15 minutes or until tender. Drain, then mix with the lemon juice, chives, yellow pepper and radishes.

2 Put the spinach leaves into shallow salad bowls, spoon the bulghur wheat on top, then add the flaked smoked mackerel. Mix the dressing ingredients together and drizzle over the fish. Finish with a grinding of black pepper.

Jasmine-brined roasted poussins with salsa verde

Brine-curing (see page 169) the poussins ensures a crispy skin when roasted. You can use any tea to make the brine, but jasmine tea infuses a floral taste into the poussins and creates a subtle flavour when cooked. Serve with the dark green salsa verde. You can also make this with Cornish game hen.

2 poussins, weighing 700g (or 1 Cornish game hen)

1 small unwaxed lemon

1 garlic clove, crushed

1 tablespoon olive oil

sea salt and freshly ground black pepper

For the brining solution

4 tablespoons jasmine tea or 4 jasmine teabags

1.5 litres boiling water

60g coarse rock salt

1 tablespoon dark brown sugar

For the salsa verde

20g fresh flat-leaf parsley leaves

20g fresh coriander leaves

20g fresh mint leaves

2 garlic cloves, finely chopped

1 tablespoon brined capers

125ml olive oil

Equipment needed

food processor

kitchen string

Serves 2

1 First make the brine. Put the jasmine tea in a large measuring jug and pour over the boiling water. Add the rock salt and sugar and stir until dissolved. Set aside to cool completely.

2 Wash and dry the poussins and put in a deep dish. Pour the cooled brine over them, cover and refrigerate for 6–8 hours.

3 When you are ready to cook, preheat the oven to 190ºC/375ºF/Gas 5.

4 Remove the poussins from the brining mixture and pat dry, removing any leftover tea leaves. Discard the brining mixture; it cannot be used again.

5 Place the poussins in a roasting tin. Zest the lemon and reserve for the salsa verde. Cut the lemon into quarters and stuff the cavities with them. Tie the legs together with kitchen string. Mix together the garlic and oil and rub over the skin of the poussins. Season with salt and pepper.

6 Roast in the preheated oven for 35 minutes until cooked and the poussin juices run clear.

7 To make the salsa verde, put all the salsa ingredients in a food processor and pulse until roughly chopped. Be careful not to over-process; you want the salsa to be slightly chunky. Season with salt and pepper.

8 When the poussins are ready, remove from the oven and set aside in a warm place to rest for 10 minutes, covered with kitchen foil. Carve and serve with the salsa verde.

Traditional fish pie

Nothing beats a steaming, creamy smoked fish pie on a cold winter's evening. The hint of mustard and boiled eggs lift this from a safe supper dish to a fantastic winner of a pie.

500ml milk

750g smoked haddock, skinned

275g unsalted butter

I tablespoon English mustard powder

4 tablespoons plain flour

2 hard-boiled eggs, peeled and quartered

Ikg floury potatoes

sea salt and freshly ground black pepper

Serves 4

1 Preheat the oven to 200°C/400°F/Gas 6.

2 Put the milk in a wide saucepan, heat just to boiling point, then add the fish. Turn off the heat and leave the fish to poach until opaque – do not over-cook.

3 Meanwhile, melt 125g of the butter in another saucepan, then stir in the mustard and flour. Remove from the heat and strain the poaching liquid into the pan.

4 Arrange the fish and eggs in a shallow pie dish or casserole.

5 Return the pan to the heat and, whisking vigorously to smooth out any lumps, bring the mixture to the boil. Season to taste, but take care because it may be salty enough. Pour the sauce into the casserole and mix carefully with the fish and eggs.

6 Cook the potatoes in boiling salted water until soft, then drain. Return to the pan. Melt the remaining 150g butter in a small pan. Reserve 4 tablespoons of this butter and stir the remainder into the potatoes. Mash well and season. Spoon the mixture carefully over the sauced fish, brush with the reserved butter and transfer to the oven. Cook for 20 minutes, or until nicely browned.

Note: If you can't find smoked haddock, you can sprinkle 125g smoked salmon, finely sliced, over poached fresh haddock just before adding the sauce.

Useful addresses

Recommended Producers

The Dairy

Cothi Valley Goats
Cilwr Farm
Tally
Llandeilo
Carmarthenshire SA19 7BQ
01558 685555

Holker Farm Dairy
Cark-in-Cartmel
Grange-over-Sands
Cumbria LA11 7PS
01539 558014
www.holkerfarm.co.uk

Ivy House Farm Dairy
Beckington
Frome
Somerset BA11 6TF
01373 831302
www.ivyhousefarmdairy.co.uk

Neal's Yard Creamery
Caeperthy
Arthur's Stone Lane
Dorstone
Herefordshire HR3 6AX
01981 500395
www.nealsyardcreamery.co.uk

The Bakery

The Bertinet Kitchen and
Bakery
12 St Andrew's Terrace
Bath BA1 2QR
01225 445531
www.bertinet.com

Long Crichel Bakery
Long Crichel
Wimbourne
Dorset BH21 5JU
01258 830852
www.longcrichelbakery.co.uk

Staff of Life Bakery
2 Berry's Yard
27 Finkle Street
Kendal
Cumbria LA9 4AB
01539 738606
www.artisanbreadmakers.co.uk

The Sweetshop

Paul A Young Fine
Chocolates
3 Camden Passage
Islington
London N1 8EA
020 7424 5750
www.paulayoung.co.uk

Sweet Treats Bakery
Parc Lodge
Llansadwn
Carmarthenshire SA19 8LW
01550 777170
www.sweettreatsbakery.co.uk

The Toffee Shop
7 Brunswick Road
Penrith
Cumbria CA11 7LU
01768 862008
www.thetoffeeshop.co.uk

William Curley
198 Ebury Street
London SW1W 8UN
020 7730 5522
and
10 Paved Court
Richmond
Surrey TW9 1LZ
020 8332 3002
www.williamcurley.co.uk

The Pantry

England Preserves
18 Druid Street
Brunswick Court
London SE1 2EY
020 7403 3380

Gringley Gringo Chilli
Products
Mayflower Cottage
Clumber Park National Park
Nr. Worksop
Nottinghamshire S80 3BQ
01909 808515
www.gringleygringo.com

Mr Todiwala Chutneys and
Pickles
16 Prescot Street
London E1 8AZ
020 7488 9242
www.mrtodiwala.com

Seafarers
Unit 3 Kemmings Close
Paignton
Devon TQ4 7TW
01803 557746
www.seafarers.net

Stratta Vinegars, Oils and
Preserves
33 Vicarage Drive
Eastbourne
East Sussex BN20 8AP
01323 732505
www.stratta.org

Wendy Brandon Preserves
Felin Wen
Boncath
Pembs SA37 0JR
01239 841568
www.wendybrandon.co.uk

The Butcher's

Baxter's Potted Shrimp
Thornton Road
Morecambe
Lancashire LA4 5PB
01524 410910
www.baxterspottedshrimps.co.uk

Lidgate's Butcher
110 Holland Park Avenue
London W11 4UA
020 7727 8243
www.lidgates.com

Trealy Farm Charcuterie
Trealy Farm
Mitchell Troy
Monmouth NP25 4BL
01600 740705
www.trealy.co.uk

The Smokehouse

Black Mountain's Smokery
Ltd
Leslie House
Elvicta Estate
Crickhowell
Powys NP8 1DF
01873 811566
www.smoked-foods.co.uk

Cley Smokehouse
High Street
Cley
Holt
Norfolk NR25 7RF
01263 740282
www.cleysmokehouse.com

Richardson's Smokehouse
Baker's Lane
Orford
Suffolk IP12 2LH
01394 450103
www.richardsonssmokehouse.
co.uk

Find a Local Food Market

FoodLovers Britain
PO Box 66303
London NW6 9PD
020 8969 0083
www.FoodLoversBritain.com

Fork2Fork
www.fork2fork.org.uk

Scottish Farmers' Markets
www.scottishfarmersmarkets.
co.uk

Certified Farmers' Markets –
FARMA
Lower Ground Floor
12 Southgate Street
Winchester
Hampshire SO23 9EF
0845 45 88 420
www.farmersmarkets.net

For further information
on farm animal welfare
standards, visit
www.rspca.org.uk/freedomfood

Index

Acknowledgements

Henrietta Green:
Thanks to all the craft producers who shared their secrets and to the staff at Cico: Cindy Richards, Gillian Haslam and Pete Jorgensen.

Jenny Linford:
My heartfelt thanks to all the food producers I talked to for their time and patience: Cothi Valley Goats, Ivy House Dairy Farm, Neal's Yard Creamery, Staff of Life, Richard Bertinet, Long Crichel, The Toffee Shop, Sweet Treats, Paul A. Young, Wendy Brandon, Seafares, England Preserves, Lidgate's, Trealy Farm, Baxter's Potted Shrimps, Black Mountains Smokery, Richardson's Smokehouse and Cley Smokehouse.

Picture credits

Key: a=above, b=below, r=right, l=left, c=centre

Martin Brigdale 42, 53bl, 54, 55al, 55ar, 60al, 60ar, 60bc, 60br, 61al, 61ar, 134, 153
Peter Cassidy 65, 66, 71l, 75, 76, 95, 101l, 102, 105, 135, 137, 138, 139, 140, 141, 154, 161, 168, 170
Gus Filgate 63
Tara Fisher 18
Jonathan Gregson 164, 171
Winfried Heinze 72, 73, 74l, 91, 96
Richard Jung 40, 48, 100, 157
Gavin Kingcome 7r, 10, 12r, 13, 14, 15, 16, 17, 19, 20, 27br, 36, 37, 38, 41, 43, 44, 45, 46, 47, 49, 51, 70, 78, 81, 104, 132, 133, 142, 143, 158, 163, 165, 167
William Lingwood 34, 181, 185
David Munns 12l

Noel Murphy 21
Gloria Nicol 92, 101r, 103, 106, 107, 108, 109, 110, 111, 125, 126, 127, 129
William Reavell 183
Claire Richardson 166
Lucinda Symons 114
Debi Treloar 31
Ian Wallace 162
Stuart West 1, 2, 4, 5, 6, 7l, 8, 9, 22, 23, 24, 25, 26, 27al, 27ar, 27bl, 28, 29, 50, 52al, 52r, 55b, 56, 57, 58, 59, 60bl, 61r, 68, 74r, 82, 83, 84, 85, 87, 88, 89, 90, 98, 112, 113, 115, 116, 117, 118, 119, 120, 121, 122, 123, 130, 144, 145, 146, 147, 148, 149, 150, 151, 169, 172, 173, 174, 175, 176, 177, 178, 179
Kate Whitaker 33, 97
Polly Wreford 71r

Recipe credits

Key: r=right, l=left

Valerie Aikman-Smith 93r, 184
Maxine Clarke 63, 95, 153, 181
Linda Collister 54, 56, 94
Ross Dobson 157
Liz Franklin 34
Henrietta Green 30, 32, 35, 52, 62, 64, 67, 116, 124r, 126, 128r, 146, 152, 155, 156, 180, 182
Rachael Anne Hill 183

Jenny Linford 22, 24, 26, 28, 58, 60, 82, 151
Hannah Miles 97
Gloria Nicol 92, 120, 122, 124l, 125, 127, 128l, 129
Louise Pickford 93l
Fiona Smith 154
Sonia Stevenson 185
Nicki Trench 84, 91, 96
Louise Wagstaffe 86, 89, 112, 118, 144, 149, 172, 174, 177, 178
Fran Warde 31
Laura Washburn 65, 66

Additional credits

Home economist: Louise Wagstaffe 22–29, 52–61 82–90, 112–123, 144–151, 172–179
Stylist: Luis Peral-Aranda 22–29, 52–61 82–90, 112–123, 144–151, 172–179